The American Immigration Collection

Culture and Democracy in the United States

HORACE M. KALLEN

Arno Press and The New York Times

NEW YORK 1970

Reprint Edition 1970 by Arno Press Inc.

Reprinted by permission of
The Liveright Publishing Corporation

LC# 72-129404
ISBN 0-405-00557-1

The American Immigration Collection—Series II
ISBN for complete set 0-405-00543-1

Manufactured in the United States of America

CULTURE AND DEMOCRACY
IN
THE UNITED STATES

CULTURE AND DEMOCRACY
IN
THE UNITED STATES

*Studies in the Group Psychology
of the American Peoples*

HORACE M KALLEN

BONI AND LIVERIGHT
PUBLISHERS   ::   ::   NEW YORK

*Acknowledgments are due to the Editors of "The
Nation," "The New Republic," "The Journal of Philosophy" and "Immigrants in America Review" for
permission to reprint essays appearing in this book.*

To
the Memory of
BARRETT WENDELL
Poet, Teacher, Man of Letters,
Deep-seeing Interpreter of America and
the American Mind,
In Whose Teaching I Received
My First Vision of Their Trends and
Meanings
I Reverently Dedicate This Book

CONTENTS

CONTENTS

POSTSCRIPT—TO BE READ FIRST

CULTURE AND THE KU KLUX KLAN

THIS book is a study in the psychology of the American peoples. It brings together a series of reflections upon the nature of culture and of democracy, upon their bearing to one another in the United States, and upon their underlying dynamics in the nationalities, the cultural traditions, the political forms, the economic pursuits, and the social and spiritual endeavors of the many peoples striving toward life, liberty and happiness amid the varied settings of the American scene.

The reflections which compose the study are occasional pieces, set down under the impact or solicitation of some special circumstance or event such as the drawing of an issue in public policy or the appearance of a new book in its field. All but one have, in somewhat different form, been printed elsewhere, often at widely separate intervals. The earliest, the discussion of the relation between democracy and "the melting pot," was written in 1914; the latest, the summary of the bearing of "Americanization" upon the pros-

pect for culture in the United States, was set
down rather less than a year ago. The others
fall between. Their composition thus covers the
period of practically a decade, a decade which
may be considered, in the history of the American mind, one of the most critical ten-year
periods that the Republic has ever passed
through. Quite explicitly, though accidentally,
the essays of this book serve to record, interpret
and register phases of the crisis. The issues with
which they deal were just coming up when the
first essay was written. The option the issues
offered was then vague and the confrontation of
the alternatives was indistinct and without pre-
vision. To-day the issues are full in the public
eye. Public sentiment has become articulated
regarding them. The option they offer is definite
and is felt to be momentous. Decision thus far,
where decision has come, has been determined by
prejudice, bubbling "reasons" from its depths to
give it decency in its own eyes. The play of
forces seeking resolution has been blind, passionate and illegitimate. Argument has been the
argument of foregone conclusions, on exactly
the sort of issues upon which no conclusion can
be foregone and be wise, no argument reasonable
and fabricated to be just that.

This situation is my excuse for bringing these
reflections together in a single book. Their in-

ward propulsion and their outward sequence do show the influence of the discontinuity of their composition. There are repetitions. There are redundancies. There are points overargued and there are points understated. For these, for the absence of that unity and movement of argument and mood which are proper to a train of thought expressed between a single pair of covers, I present my apologies. For the matter itself none are required and none are offered. Each essay is an attack along a different radius on the center of the same theme. The progressions of thought turn out, I venture to think, to be concentric and convergent, so that the book may present to the reader a unity at least of attitude, substance and philosophy which, I hope, will a little compensate for its otherwise deficient form.

The standpoint of these essays can be described briefly as Cultural Pluralism. The outcome of the observations they embody is the view that democracy is an essential prerequisite to culture, that culture can be and sometimes is a fine flowering of democracy, and that the history of the relation of the two in the United States exhibits this fact.

So old-fashioned a teaching is at the present time popular nowhere in the United States. Both American tories and American intellectuals reject it. They reject it because they find themselves all at once undermined in all their customary securities—in their securities of habit, of thought, of outlook—by the shift of the social facts upon which the securities were postulated. And they have taken sides accordingly.

The story of their partisanship and conflict is one of the recurrent ironies in the confused tale of the American mind. It is the gigantic irony in the adventure of culture in the United States. What brought them to light and leading is the Great War. This sharply transformed the fission of class feeling into a gulf between the classes: the growing uneasiness of the native-born in the presence of the immigrant from an unconscious strain into a conscious repulsion, the condescending certainty of native superiority into an alarmed proclamation of it, and the naïve assurance that it cannot be otherwise into frenzied argument that it must be sheltered to survive. Hundreds of associations, from the National Security League to the Ku Klux Klan, were formed to sustain its status and guard its privileges. These associations are to-day vested interests of the communities whose life is their propaganda, and whose propaganda is a cry to hereditary prejudice and privilege that their position is no longer secure. The cry has many voices, but one burden. Whether in the

general Know Nothingism of the attack against
the foreign-born for being foreign-born, or in the
general alarm of exploiting capital in the attack
against liberal practice and opinion in politics
or the economic life, or in the general passion of
debate in the attack of traditional religious orthodoxy against the compenetration of science
and higher criticism with religion which is called
modernism, the burden is the same: *The old
values that rule the common life are in danger.
Arm, arm, lest they be destroyed.*

The Great War with tanks and planes and poison gas has been followed by a battle of values,
of norms and standards; a struggle of theories of
life. And it was the Great War which brought
the battle on. That this event should bring the
battle on was inevitable. As a battle is a crisis
in a war, so a war is a crisis in a history. A crisis
brings to focus and to resolution a chronic process
the changes in which are cumulative, the apex and
termination of the cumulus consisting in a new
direction, a new rhythm and a new pattern for
the energies of the group life. The Great War
constituted such a crisis in the politico-economic
process of the life of nations. One arrangement
of the forces confronting each other in the process has been reduced and absorbed. It is not
yet apparent—indeed, the recent history of Europe would seem to point to the opposite con-

clusion—but it is true nevertheless that, for better or worse, the activities of nations have been redirected in a channel of ideas toward a pattern of federalism imposed by the energies and required by the forms of the economy of machine industry. Prior to this economy, both in time and in logic, reënforcing it and by it reënforced, is the subtle, irresistible, all-penetrating influence of the outlook and technique of science.

The two together, science and industry, touching the American scene and the American mind here and there, and again there and here, brought it into contact with a whole world of miscellaneous influences, ethnic, cultural, economic, social, religious, scientific, literary and graphic. For more than a generation the impact, compenetration and rearrangement of the old and new elements of American life into untraditional patterns took place as a process felt, but unseen and unchallenged. Toward the end of the first decade of the century, the feeling, which had hitherto received expression in over-emphatic gratulation, took form in uneasiness and got utterance in alarm. Ethnic contrasts began to be made, cultural comparisons, sociological special pleas. Before these beginnings could run their course in public discussion, generating their appropriate anti-bodies of argument in the blood of public opinion and terminating without danger to the

health of the body-politic, the Great War came
up, dividing the land, intensifying and focalizing
passions, and finally, with America's entry
therein, converting this whole, relatively smooth,
slow process of change into a thing rapid, sudden, explosive and—dangerous; a thing articulated in a collection of dogmas which stated definite issues and causes for the public mind. These
dogmas are at bottom no more than verbal pre-
cipitates of strong emotions, emotions which
began as uneasiness and which the War lashed
into fear and jealousy—fear lest the current
values of privilege and prejudice be dethroned;
jealousy of what seem to be their ostensible successors.

Under circumstances such as these, in which
physical effort is outspanned only by psychological tension, and emotions run high without run-
ning free and thus of themselves purge the
spirit of the people, all the established ways of
life suffer shock and are shaken. Habits of work
and of feeling are loosened. Instabilities of temper appear where none or little had been seen
before. Institutions, beliefs, philosophies, seem
together on a verge. Terror grows lest they
should topple. Men rush to their defense. They
cease to take, as was their wont and use, the existence of these for granted. Foundations and

superstructures are reëxamined, worths reassessed. Everything comes under review, and prevailingly issue is joined concerning the usually unconsidered premise implicit in all social attitudes. This premise relates to the constancy or variability of human nature. If the turbulence of the times within you takes form in a discontent of hope, it makes of you an optimist, a revolutionary, a perfectionist. Change human nature! Why, of course. And for the better always. Day by day, in every way, for the better, if only change can be free. If, on the other hand, the turbulence of the times within you takes form in a discontent of fear, if change seems loss and destruction, it makes of you a pessimist, a conservative. You insist on clinging to what you have. You refuse to barter *Is* for *May be.* What, change human nature! How can you? As it was in the beginning, so must it be in the days to come, forever and ever, Amen. That your latter end may be no worse than your beginning, your nature and heritage must be not other than in the beginning. You stake your all upon immobility and wage war upon time and change.

It is such a challenge and review that the Great War brought into action in the United States. It converted interpenetration into confrontation, dislocation into conflict. The gener-

ations that since the Civil War had been making
the new America had taken what men and what
materials served their needs in what ways reached
their felt goals best, heedless of the unforeseen
consequences to themselves, to the American
scene, to the American spirit. It was wealth
they wanted, and power they wanted. It was
railroads they built and mills—steel mills, flour
mills, cotton and woolen mills—they erected, for
the sake of the wealth, for the sake of the power.
For the sake of the wealth and power they drew
the peoples of Europe and Asia to these shores.
They used them and they scrapped them as they
used and scrapped natural resources, legislative
agents, social and political decencies. They got
wealth and power. They made America great.
But their instrumentalities and their ends had
each their by-products, by-products of social and
intellectual life, by-products of culture. The
new material America began to grow a new
America of the spirit. The character and com-
plexion of the body-politic, transformed by the
economic adventure, disturbed the traditional national outlook; by absorbing and generating new
elements of force and feeling they broke up and
confused such unity as pertained to the national
mind.

This mind was a simple enough thing in its
time. Its forward prospect was the domination

of the virgin continent; its inheritance, its treasure of memory and values, was a tradition of culture and cultus transplanted from Europe and having its social focus in the institutions of the church. The forward prospect was the concern of the men of the land. The cultural tradition was left largely to its women. Only under the roof of the evangelical church were the sexes joined in a common spiritual concern. But the men went out from the church into a life of another dimension, into the adventure of the pioneer in field or mine or counting house or factory. The women went out from the church into the adventure of the pioneer in culture.

For though the church dominated, it could not hold, either sex. Beginning with an unmitigated and unquestioned authority over everything, it had ended with authority only in the field of the familial *mores* that might on occasion come scandalously under the public eye. Its outlook was too barren, its practice too starved, to restrain the imagination from the rich adventures of business freely competitive, of culture freely predigested, fantastic and decorative. Both were escapes from the drabness of the primal evangelical puritanism. One was attained through the type of association known as the woman's club. In this, with all its pretense, superficiality and hokum, women found release and relief from the dull compulsions of the daily life. It was their gate to the other world, heard of, but hardly ever seen, of wisdom, gayety and serious beauty. It opened out upon these things even though it did not open into them. And they were by women pronounced and proclaimed to be alone the realities.

The escape from the coercive drab tradition which business offered lacked these attributes. It was conflict. It was adventure. It was speed and it was urgency. But it was no purge for accumulated feeling through gayety and wisdom and serious beauty. Its actions were too comminuted; its tenseness of competition too nerve-racking; its agonists were too much alone. The men of America, as men everywhere, also needed fellowship and purgative communication. They found it—for that matter, they seem still to find it—in the great fraternal secret orders. These were to the men what their clubs were to the women. And more. Their attributes had the mysterious communion of religion. They supplemented the church, supplying what evangelical Christianity lacked—the color, the ritual, the strong feeling of fellowship, the mystery. "Elks," "Moose," "Eagles," "Redmen," "Shriners," "Masons," "Western Stars," "Odd Fellows," and so on, present in name, ritual and practice the characteristics of the great totemic

societies of the simpler peoples, gathered to cele-
brate with due rite their fellowship in god, their
own proper god, and in one another. Channels
for feeling roused by the daily life but without
avenues of expression in the traditional institutions of the daily life, the secret orders took their
place with the women's clubs as supplements to
the evangelical church. Their existence insured
the continuance of the church—which would
otherwise have undergone considerable mutation
—relatively unchanged, and the unchanged sanction of familial habit which is the stuff of the
irony pertaining to the Main Street.

The prevailing emotional tone of the American of this period was one of self-assurance rising swiftly to self-glorification. Contagion from
the prosperous economic enterprise of the nation
was not without large influence on this feeling.
There went with it a vast resilient faith, a confidence in the excellence of the American being and
the happy outcome of American undertakings.
Whatever was thought contributory to these was
the theme of gratulatory comment—science, in-
vention, work, smartness, neighborliness. America was the land of opportunity, of goodwill, of
the free field and much favor for each man, who
could make of himself what he would. A naïve
pride of race and cult, attested socially in the
rise of numerous social and religious historical

societies and an identification of personal success
with national progress, went with it.[1] Optimistic emotion engendered by the urgent adventure
of the winning of the continent absorbed all the
contradictions in the American scene and pro-
jected an image of the "typical American," puritan and pioneer, sentimental and ruthless, snob
and democrat, cock of the roost with Fortunatus'
cap on his head, sitting pretty on the top of the
world and whistling "Yankee Doodle."   Him
travelers from the East used to be so amused at,
irritated with and disgusted by,[2] and he figured
as the ideal self that each American youth might
become if he were good. The great anxiety, the
great race and quarrel of the land, was over property. Waves of social antagonism and religious
hatred swept it and subsided. Alien groups, first
opposed, then exploited, then accepted, were one
after another acclimated to the social temper and
more or less stably settled in the community of
the United States. Only with respect to the
Negro was there a steady and cumulative antagonism, and that is due as much, perhaps, to the
negro's having been property and to the holding

[1] Compare the late Col. Roosevelt to Mr. Edward Bok: "We
must work together for the same end, you in your way, I in
mine. But our lines are bound to cross. You and I can each
become good Americans by giving our best to make America
better. With the Dutch stock there is in both of us, there's no
limit to what we can do. Let's go to it." (*The Americanization
of Edward Bok*, pp. 266-67.)

[2] J. G. Brooks, *As Others See Us.*

over of the traditional attitude toward private
property in private feeling and public policy.
Property in things, under the deepening impress
of industrialism, became to the owners of things
the first principle of Americanism, and the confrontation of common welfare with private own-
ership grew to be, and remains, the major constitutional issue in the law of the land. In the
course of time it was summed up by the slogan
of the abortive progressive movement: "human
rights versus property rights." When this movement was at the crest, the hopefulness of America
regarding mankind was at its highest. The
"melting pot" was predestined to make a successful and happy American—that is, a man of
property—of any one. Witness Mr. Bok, Mr.
Pupin, Miss Antin, Mr. Riis, Mr. Steiner, and
scores of others vocal, and thousands of still
others, propertied but dumb.

At the same time the sons and the daughters
of the women who manned the clubs and made
of the life of the spirit in the United States a
window toward Europe came of age and, after
the manner of the young, demanded a cultural
ménage of their own, in their own right. This
demand was nothing new. It was a literary tradition of America, from the first public sigh after
"the great American novel" and Whitman's

"Literatus," to the endeavors upon American themes in the verse and prose of the New England School of europeanizers—Myles Standish, Evangeline, Knickerbocker, Amos Bigelow, Silas Lapham. But this American thing was, in the tradition, to be autochthonous, a growth of the soil, born of its potencies, not its rejections. The newer generation, whose most competent critical voice was perhaps Mr. Van Wyck Brooks, was all for a declaration of cultural independence, a throwing off of Europe, and a fresh, free, cultural start. The exclusions were at least as important as the inclusions, and of the latter there could be great hope.

Such, by and large, were the process and direction of change among the business men and the club women of the North American Republic prior to the Great War. Such were their anxieties and hopes. What this war did was to turn the anxiety about property into one about people. It now became people, qualities of race, heritage and attitude, not law, which was the menace to property and to the status it signified. What the war did was to turn the anxiety about the independence of American culture into a despair about its existence. The American scene, the culturemen declared, could breed no culture. A man of skill and spirit, to save them alive, must abandon America and live abroad. Culture in the United States was like snakes in Ireland.

A widespread hysterical taking of stock began. Immigration, formerly more than welcomed as an economic boon, was now scrutinized as a eugenic menace. The stuff and form of the American being were reëxamined, not by visitors from abroad any longer, but by scared lodgers at home. Racial theories were promulgated descanting variously upon the magical superiority of the Nordic stock. In the decade 1914-1924 a succession of manifestos appeared, each painting a blacker and blacker picture, until finally, the faint new patterns of association generated by the industrial development of the United States were represented as an assault upon civilization. An appearance of scientific precision and mathematical certainty was imparted to the jeremiads by the statistical tables culled from the "intelligence tests," army and civilian. The army ones were fabricated by psychologists serving in the American army during the Great War. Their purpose was to enable the selection of eligible officers in the shortest possible time. They were not concerned about the strength of the abilities they were testing for —they were concerned about the relative order of the abilities they were testing for. The standards by which the abilities were measured were intrinsic to the measurements themselves and to their special purposes, and therefore incommensurable with any others. What, broadly, the tables exhibited, was a correlation between "native" Americans of position and importance, with habituation in the use of the English language and the positions which, on the whole, such Americans hold. From this exhibition, which is a foregone conclusion, fear and vanity both drew their class and group confirmation. Fear, because the "inferior" stocks were declared to be increasing so much more rapidly than the "superior," and, like the proverbial camel, crowding the master out of the tent. Vanity, because the "intelligence quotients" were inferred to demonstrate that the "upper" classes are so by original nature and not by institutional accident. In them the excellence of mankind was held to be automatically concentrated.[1] The argument had of course the circular character of all such arguments. Its archetype is the Brahminical explanation of the Brahmins of India that they are the highest caste because they sprang from the head of Brahma and they

[1] Cf. W. MacDougall: *Is America Safe for Democracy?*; C. C. Brigham: *A Study of American Intelligence*; L. Stoddard: *The Assault on Civilization*, and *The Rising Tide of Color*. The parent of all these alarums and excursions seems to be H. S. Chamberlain's *Grundzüge des Neunzehnten Jahrhunderds*. Chamberlain's racial fantasies were, so far as I know, first restated in the United States with American implications by Mr. Madison Grant, in *The Passing of the Great Race*.

know that they sprang from the head of Brahma because they are the highest caste.

In this use of the army intelligence tests evidence to the contrary that they themselves contain was either ignored or belittled. The difference in success with the tests arising from a knowledge of the English language, the difference between native-born and immigrant generations of the same stock, the very important difference that time made, the practical impossibility of selecting out and isolating the hereditary factor in "intelligence," the variability and indefiniteness of that concept itself, the tremendous importance of the environmental influences of infancy, the rôle of social status, temperament, education and innumerable other factors, were ignored or belittled. The scales used in intelligence tests generally were assumed to be of universal validity when, in fact, the record showed at least twenty-four different revisions of the Binet-Simon scale alone, revisions having reference to the selection of the tests and the designation of the age group to which a given test might apply.[1] Because, on a given scale the average "intelligence quotient" of the army recruits was that of children about thirteen years old on another scale, the inference was swiftly drawn that the "mental age" of the United States was

[1] Cf. Cyril Burt: *Mental and Scholastic Tests.*

about thirteen years, and that the country was
going to the dogs, i.e., to the immigrants.
Where there was any hitch in the figures, they
were manipulated, as by Mr. Brigham, to make
them prove the case for vanity and fear. Where
a careful scrutiny of them might make the opposite demonstration, they were ignored, as by
Mr. MacDougall, to whom the premise that "the
upper social strata as compared with the lower
contain a larger proportion of persons of superior
natural endowments" was a proposition emotion-
ally ineffable. That on the most liberal interpretation of the army records this could not be
so, given the relative numerical proportions of
"upper" and "lower" "social strata," was not
even speculated upon. The postulate of "natural
superiority" of the "upper social strata" was a
prior assumption. Its roots were in feeling, not
in observation, and the demonstration of it could
be nothing more than a dialectical elaboration
of itself, the rationalization of a prejudice seeking to pass itself off as a judgment.

This prejudice is the natural spontaneous
prejudice of a social class in its own favor.
Given its privileges and its position, given the
challenge to them which the Great War made
clear, what else could follow, in its mobilization
of its intellectual defenses, than a view of human nature by which qualities conventionally

regarded as superior—such as intelligence—shall
be fixed and invariant in character and in quantity, and that they shall be distributed in such
a way that the privileged shall be privileged by
merit and not by accident, and that they shall
be justified in retaining their privileges by inherent nature and not by force? From the head
of Brahma sprang they; where, then, in the social
order, can their place be, save at the head?

The literature of race in which the current
capitalist apologetics took form had its foil of
course. Not merely were its contentions not permitted to pass unchallenged, but they were subjected to a thoroughgoing analysis which completely demolished their logical foundations, even
though they remained afterward, standing as
firmly as ever.[1] For what they stand on, it cannot be too often emphasized, is not the observations and inferences arising out of a scientific survey of human quality but the passions and prejudices arising out of the disturbed state of mind
of a social class grown fearful of the security of
its status.

The irony of this situation gets a richer
savor by the fact that just at the time when
Weismannism and Mendelism are most invoked
to justify and eternalize the god of things as

---

[1] Cf. Walter Lippmann's articles on the Intelligence Tests in
The New Republic and Mr. Cyril Burt's book, already referred to.

they are, scientific investigation both in biology
and in psycho-physiology once more seriously
raises the question whether the dogma, that acquired characteristics cannot be inherited, is more
than what wise biologists use it as—a methodo-
logical convenience by which biological combi-
nations may be more or less mathematically cal-
culated. There are the experiments of the Aus-
trian Kammerer, on the salamander and the ascidian. There are the experiments of Griffith
and Guyer, Americans, on rats and rabbits.
There are the experiments of the great Russian,
Pawlow, on white mice. The experiments on
the salamander and the ascidian, on the rat and
the rabbit, make a *prima facie* case, the importance of which cannot be seriously questioned,
for the inheritance of acquired physical traits.
The experiments upon the white mice make an
even more significant case for the inheritance
of acquired "mental" traits.

Pawlow is primarily a physiologist whose re-
searches led him into psychology. He has laid
bare a vital process whose study and use have
been the most fertilizing activity known to psychologists of the present generation. This process is called "the conditioned reflex." Upon it
what is most scientific in modern psychology has
been built. By means of it the most obscure psychological event can be cleared up and simplified,

whether this event be conceived in the patterns of Dr. Freud's "unconscious" or Dr. Watson's "behavior." A reflex is "conditioned" when it is released or touched off not merely by its spontaneous natural stimulus, but by anything present in close association with this stimulus. Thus, the appearance of food will automatically bring a flow of saliva into the mouth. If at the same time that the food appears a bell should be rung, then, after an interval, the ringing of that bell will of itself produce a flow of saliva. The bell becomes a substitute and symbol for the food, and the symbol evokes the same response as the thing symbolized. Pawlow conditioned the salivary response of white mice to a bell. He bred the conditioned mice for several generations. The record of the behavior of the generations shows that the first generation required three hundred stimulations before it established a conditioned reflex, that the second generation required only one hundred stimulations, and the fourth no more than ten. Pawlow thinks that in the course of time white mice might make a salivary response to the sound of a bell directly, at birth, just as chickens peck at spots directly they emerge from the shell. Between "the conditioned reflex" and intelligence there exists an intimate organic connection not unlike that between foundation and superstructure.

Man is an animal whose chief distinction is his possession and use of language, of signs and symbols. That is, man is an animal whose conditioned reflexes are indefinitely manifold. And "intelligence" is intimately involved in the existence and use of conditioned reflexes.

Need the ironic implications of the discoveries of the great Pawlow for the rationalizations of their status by the spokesmen of the privileged class that compose the apologia of privilege be elaborated?

Human nature, these discoveries imply, is variable and viable. So far as it is a going concern, there are no inevitables, no rigidities, in it, whether of "intelligence," feeling or habit. Literally and figuratively it makes headway, even in the United States. This is especially apparent in the history of the spirit of man, in the world at large, and in America particularly. That accounting of the stock of civilization which began during the Great War in the mutual recriminations between the Germans and the Allies, developed after it in a generic encyclopædism of history, of the sciences of the arts.[1] The passionate interests of men shifted from the endeavors of business to the analysis of mind. The hysteria about the intelligence tests was only one aspect

[1] Cf. the procession of "Outlines" that was led by Mr. H. G. Wells' *Outline of History.*

of this common preoccupation. Men showed
themselves to have lost their certainties about
themselves, about their destinies. In this region, too, they became anxious or despairful
about the old securities and sought to reëstablish
them by force or to reject them by knowledge
or by laughter. The self-styled younger generation assess civilization in the United States
and find it a wanting puritanism. An older
generation takes up arms on behalf of this puritanism as a doctrine and discipline of the good
life. There is much noisy disputation and more
blind seeking. Men desire a map of life again.
They want a philosophy, they want a religion.
How much they want it can be seen from the
swiftness and the urgency with which religion,
before the Great War crowded more and more
to the periphery of public affairs, has swung
back into their center. The issue suddenly so
vital between "fundamentalism" and "modernism" gets its force from this feeling of insecurity and the fear it arouses. The indignation with
evolution has no other motive. The final manifestation in the Ku Klux Klan has no other
source.

In none of the confrontations here enumerated can the antagonists be said to have anything
new in their hearts. Essentially, the relations
that obtain between them have always obtained.

But before the Great War they were passive rather than active. The new was suffusing and displacing the old, continuously, imperceptibly, surely. Irrevocably it was building a new America, an America of new institutions, new stocks, new ideals, with a richer and more varied cultural inheritance and therefore cultural prospect. Then a thing happened not unlike the thing that happened to Christian Europe when Luther the monk turned the gradual displacements of the Renaissance into the swift antagonisms of the Reformation. Old things dying began to feel themselves die and to struggle against death. The passions of such a struggle are often courage in the individual, but in groups and communities, they are fear and hatred. Thus, the vindicators of the old, the traditional, the tried assurances of faith and hope, evince a depth of rancorous passion without parallel among the exponents of the newer ways. This feeling it is which has been added to the old differences. It is this that flames in the fiery cross of the Ku Klux Klan.

The Klan, indeed, is the concretion, sublimate, and gratification of the passions in play since the coming of the Great War. It is most representative of the convulsive effort of the orders at ease in the Zion of the old ways and standards of life in the United States to keep back the dissolution which industry and science and democracy condemn them to. Its membership is recruited from every class and every station in the United States that considers itself "native, white and Protestant." Its animating hate extends to everything that, like Jew, Catholic or negro, is a variant from this type by traditional opinion, or that, like views of minorities upon religion, politics, economics, manners or morals, is a variant from the conventional type by recorded utterance or act. What, however, is stressed by the Klan for castigation, and how, differs largely from locality to locality. It is all covered, nevertheless, by the conglomerate of conventional values according to which the United States is assumed to live. Definiteness such values cannot, of course, have. Time, place, and circumstances of hatred specify them. As Brother Edward Clarke Young, Imperial Wizard Pro Tem proclaimed in September, 1922, "to all Klans and Klansmen and to American citizens Who Believe in Their Country and Want to See Its Every Interest Protected, the Knights of the Ku Klux Klan has been organized for the purpose of safeguarding and protecting these things in and for America which are fundamental to the greatness of the Nation, are the things for which our Fathers fought and died to preserve and perpetuate in America. . . .

The Knights of the Ku Klux Klan, now thoroughly organized and entrenched in every corner of the United States, is determined to keep faith with America and Americans. . . . It does here and now declare war to the bitter end upon all those in America who are seeking in an insidious but powerful manner to undermine the very fundamentals of the Nation."

Neither the "fundamentals of the Nation" nor that which is "seeking to undermine" them have any counterpart of reality, of fact or event in the minds of the writer and readers of this gem of southern English style. The phrases stand for attitudes, for emotions, and the actualities toward which the attitudes are taken and to which the emotions attach are protean in nature and station. Their variety is as endless as the local jealousies, superstitions, suppressed hungers and active fears and hatreds, all anti-social, that, across this broad and goodly land, have received from the Klan theology an ethical imperative which socializes them and sets them free in the Klan practice. Withal, this practice retains and underscores the mummery of communion characteristic of the older benevolent secret orders. These last, it is apparent, great improvement over the ritual of the evangelical churches though their rituals had been, had become too stale and customary, were too little in-

volved with intense feeling, not to bore. Their
ideal and practice lacked interest. They engaged
no profoundly moving passion. Such passion as
they did engage was dissipated in a general good
will, at best not a strong bond for anxious men.
The Klan, however, generates and is sustained by
fear and its consequential hates. These were
the emotions most massive and dynamic during
the Great War and immediately thereafter, and
the Klan prolongs them into the small peace
and by attaching them to certain traditional
symbols of ritual and ratiocination, institution-
alizes them. The Klan is thus the medium
wherewith greatly diverse classes utter and pro-
ject a common fear and the hatred born of it,
directing them upon this or that social movement, religious doctrine, scientific opinion or
racial group and finally fusing the anarchic diversity of these many objects of hatred into a
single hieroglyph to be described as "seeking in
an insidious but powerful manner to undermine
the fundamentals of the Nation."

An organization driven by such passions and
draining them by such behavior as the Klan's
cannot bore. Moreover, its mummery and ritual
belong, anthropologically, with the initiatory and
sacrificial rites having their origins in prehistory.
Its behaviour and program admit one to power
without responsibility. There is magic in them,

as of a fairy tale unexpectedly realized. They
enable persons often otherwise adult to revert
to infancy without losing face. Infantilism, indeed, and its fascinations are among the more
interesting manifestations of Kukluxitis, and the
connection of reversion to infancy with fear is
notorious. Think of it!—to be a knight cham-
pion, dedicated to the deliverance of a democracy in danger, by membership in an invisible empire, peopled by Wizards, Giants, Cyclops,
Kligrapps, Kleagles, Emperors, Klaptraps,
Klumps, Klimps and Klools!—to go about, under
mysterious orders from such mysterious masters,
shrouded in white, seeing but unseen, behind a
cross on fire!—to break and enter, to whip, to
shoot, to shatter, to slaughter, to tar and feather,
to burn alive!—to talk a mysterious language,
so like the hog-latin and the other invented
tongues of childhood! And to be able to be and
to enjoy all this under a theological imperative
which makes of you a savior of your church and
country, a soldier at once of the flag and the cross!

Are you a Baptist or Methodist parson—or
a parson of whatever evangelical sect—doing the
Lord's work in an empty and dilapidated church
on the Main Street, at a wage which enables your
wife to have consumption as well as children,
and your children to go to school unshod and
in cut-down garments, and yourself to get a new

overcoat once in five years if you are lucky; then, if you find all at once that your church gets filled even if the sermon is antiquated, that the roof is mended, that occasional bits of money are brought in by masked men marching behind a cross in flames, and that your stock in Gopher Prairie has somehow gone up, how can you fail to welcome the Klan? How for you, who had been cast down and are now exalted, can the Klan be other than the holy instrument of the Lord's work, a new engine of his salvation in troublous times! Can you yourself reject the opportunity it brings you, should you become a minister of its gospel as well? After all, are not the gospels of the Klan and the Christ one gospel? Have not Wizard and Giant and Emperor so proclaimed? And who shall deny it? Evolutionists, atheists, Catholics, Jews, Negroes, modernists, socialists, bolsheviks, mere writers and teachers? Fie! You become a member of the Klan and are a boy again with the boys, but this time, in righteousness, and for His Name's Sake, Amen. And you are living out childhood dreams of power and mystery.

Are you a keeper of the general store, postmaster, real estate operator, money-lender, and is the Jew across the way taking the bread out of your mouth by lending money at easier rates and with less red tape, then . . . Is it necessary

to count up the classes whose repressed anti-social
emotions the Klan liberates and socializes and
sustains with a lofty moral imperative? These
classes compose a true cross-section of what the
Imperial Wizard Pro Tem means by "American." They are in all the strata of the society of
the United States. Their ways, before the coming of industry, have been the ways of the land.
Now that the land is changing its ways, they
are afraid and they are fighting it as men afraid
always fight, with blindness and folly.   For
many, and these are the masterful financial and
industrial interests, the Klan is an instrument,
spontaneously grown to their hands, which, as
in Texas and Oklahoma, they know how to use
toward their own ends. For those among whom
it has grown spontaneously it is a liberating
evangel (in fact a fear-born crusade against the
hallucinations which fear generates). There is
a Quixotism in it, a sordid and degraded Quixotism, without grace, without kindness. When
the emotion which the Klan utters will subside,
the Klan will pass. It is not without an ancestry in the history of culture in the United
States, and it is predestined by psychological
law to share the oblivion of its forerunners.
What a trail, however, its passing will leave of
cruelty and hypocrisy, of sentimentalism and
avarice, of patriotism masking crime, of brutal-

ity dressed up as piety and of sensuality as virtue! It is the stuff that Klansmen are made of that Mr. Edward Bok must have had in mind when he wrote: "When I look around at the American-born I have come to know as my close friends, I wonder whether, after all, the foreign-born does not make in some sense a better American." [1]

Americans themselves, Mr. Bok allows himself with others to declare, are first in need of Americanization. What he means by Americanization, other than behaving like a Dutchman on the make in America, he nowhere explicitly states. He leaves you to infer that the substance of it may lie in Roosevelt's formula, that you can "become a good American by giving your best to make America better," and that your ancestral stock is a fundamental in the quality of your giving. Roosevelt's meaning, as his later conduct showed, was something rather different from what his words imply. That which they imply is not without its foundations in the political vision set forth in the Declaration of Independence and the social outlook which is harmonious with economic and political individualism. Individualism, integrity of spirit, indeed, is the heart of the matter, and its conception and definition and working are essential to the right

[1] *The Americanization of Edward Bok*, p. 451.

apprehension of whatever is precious in democracy. The Rooseveltian exhortation logically implies this. The Rooseveltian practice irrevocably repudiates it, and the Klan is a kind of Rooseveltian *massenmensch*. Its demand is not for the conservation of personality, for freedom of variation, for the ordering of institutions so as to insure to men's souls their autonomy and integrity. The Klan requires that individuality shall be submerged in conformity, that conformity shall be blind, and shall fall continuously in with the unseen and imprevisible changes of the ancestral conventions and *mores* of the American village community as these are appreciated and understood by the masters of this community. On the record, the Klan seeks social and intellectual conformity and economic and political rascality. Such an objective, brought in reflection down to its primary logical postulates and up to its ultimate social consequences, would eventuate in a philosophy of *Kultur*. Unopposed, it would render culture impossible in the United States. Its persistence from the beginning has been one of the most powerful obstructions to the prosperous development of American culture.

Fortunately, it has never existed unopposed. There is a culture in the United States and not an ignoble one. Its existence is founded upon just the things the Ku Klux Klan and Mr.

Bok's American friends as they write themselves down in the *Saturday Evening Post* reject and fight against. It is founded upon variation of racial groups and individual character; upon spontaneous differences of social heritage, institutional habit, mental attitude and emotional tone; upon the continuous, free and fruitful cross-fertilization of these by one another. Within these Many, gathered upon the American scene from the four corners of the earth and taking root and finding nourishment, growth and integrity upon its soil, lies the American One, as poets, painters, musicians and philosophers feel and utter this One.

From the days when the New England school first turned its heart to Europe for spiritual sustenance and workmanlike guidance to the days when all the cultural enclaves of Europe began to make a new life upon the North American continent, the culture of the United States has gathered volume and headway; has gathered variety, color and significance. It has gathered them because, regardless of the compulsions toward conformity that have periodically swept like tides over the nation, the spacious continent has permitted the spontaneous self-rooting and automatic growth of differentiated communities and the free flow, impact, compenetration and reordering of spiritual values between them. It

has gathered them because in the spaces of the
continent democracy could not but prevail, and
the lives of cultural groups retain their integri-
ties even as the lives of individual spirits.

This democracy—in character and constitution
social and intellectual rather than political—for
its principle is, not one man one vote, but one
temperament, one point of view, one vote—is
that which is to-day at stake in the United States.
It lies—as the history of the culture of any land
makes amply clear—at the foundation of culture
everywhere. It is the indispensable prerequisite
to the existence and growth of culture in the
United States. In manyness, variety, differen-
tiation, lies the vitality of such oneness as they
may compose. Cultural growth is founded upon
Cultural Pluralism. Cultural Pluralism is possible only in a democratic society whose institutions encourage individuality in groups, in persons, in temperaments, whose program liberates
these individualities and guides them into a fellowship of freedom and coöperation. The alternative before Americans is **Kultur Klux Klan
or Cultural Pluralism.**

I

A MEANING OF AMERICANISM [1]

WORDS may be broadly divided into two classes
—those that stand predominantly for ideas or
things and those that stand predominantly for attitudes, moods, emotions. No word, not even the
nakedest symbol of the mathematician nor the
emptiest gurgle of the popular song-writer,
stands purely for one thing or the other; each is
hyphenated, and in each a meaning and a mood
interpenetrate. The word "Americanism" is no
exception, and its character involves this interpenetration to a very high degree. Its meaning,
however—or rather one aspect or another of its
meaning—is articulate and precise only to a
thoughtful few: to the man on the street it expresses a mood, potent, excellent, desirable; to
him the distinction between "American" and
"un-American" is the distinction between good
and evil; but he cannot tell when pressed
what *is* American, and what *is* un-American—he

[1] *The Immigrants in America Review*, January, 1916, pp. 12-19.
Printed as *"The* Meaning of Americanism."

can only feel, dumbly, ineffably, that some actions
and ideals are approvable by that term and others are not, and this is the end of the story.
These actions and ideals, occurring in the same
person at the same or different times, may be each
other's exact opposites. Their practical and
logical relationships may be profoundly in conflict, and they themselves in rapid change. The
mood will nevertheless unite them, give them the
only continuity they possess, or more deeply, reflect a continuity they contain. It is in the latter
possibility alone that any hope lies of crystalliz-
ing into some form of statement a thing at once
so diffuse and organic, so protean and continuous
as that cluster of attitudes and ideals that goes
by the name "Americanism."

Now ideals possess a duality peculiar to themselves. On the one hand they may measure the
distance between what is and what is wished for;
they may formulate our reaction *against* the actual world and yield us compensation in idea for
its shortcomings in fact. Or again, they may envisage the actual process of our life and express
its potencies and character. The difference between the compensatory and expressive aspect of
ideals is determined by our behavior with regard
to them. If we rest in them, merely denying by
virtue of having conceived them, the realities
which they contradict, they are compensatory.

Then a serious danger lurks in them. They are arrestive of growth, they inhibit that process of the utilization and control of nature and the harmonization of men which we call civilization. The ideals of the dark ages were prevailingly compensatory. In the main, however, even compensatory ideals tend less to be imaginings to rest in, pleasant substitutes for unpleasant facts, than programs to work out. Our chief and necessarily dominant concern is with the future. We live forward only, and all the engines of the common life, of industry, art, religion and science, are intended to determine the channels and specify the character in which the future shall come. Actual ideals are programs of conduct in a world yet to be discovered; they are routings over an uncharted country; foresights of a still unlived life.

A commonwealth's explicit and overt ideals, consequently, are its directive soul; the standard-giving factors of its actual life. They stand, regardless of all perversion, regardless of appropriation by special classes in defense or prosecution of their special interests or manipulation in behalf of invisible and nefarious power or privilege, for what the nation as a whole conceives itself as being or as liking to be. They may be facts, they may be illusions, but in so far as they are acknowledged at all, they operate directively, and exercise a certain control over the interest that uses them for its private gain. This is true whether or not one accepts the theory of economic determinism in history, for economic determinism simply makes one set of ideals—those dealing with the indispensable fundamentals which keep life at least at its fighting weight—more important than others, but does not destroy their ideality; because we live forward, even materialism is an ideal to be abandoned or persisted in. The ideals of any society envisage the aspects of its life it prides itself upon, in so far as they are expressive, and the aspects of its life it resents and would alter, in so far as they are compensatory. The dynamics of a national life are to be sought rather in the interplay of ideal and condition than in the description of condition, and the positive program of a country tends to be more intelligible in terms of its resentments than in terms of its acceptances. No hard and fast line can be drawn between actually operative compensatory and expressive ideals; neither matter much unless they are programmatic. And consequently, to formulate the ideals of the United States, it becomes necessary to seek what has been continuously overt as program in the various enterprises which compose the biography of the land. That alone can define its explicit personality and typify its character.

This continuity of vision is designated by three words. Each has changed in meaning since it was first used to formulate a program and express a need, but its change has been a growth, analogous to the change in a human individual as he passes from childhood to maturity; involving, with all its varying, both an enrichment and a fixation. All three have been more or less implicit potencies of the national life from the outset. Each was emphasized in turn against the pressure of events and against the others. As Barrett Wendell shows, they are, in the order of their domination of the national life (1) Liberty, (2) Union, and (3) Democracy.[1]

The ideal of Liberty emerges against a background of commercial rivalry and political friction with England. The potent population of the thirteen original colonies were, at the time when Patrick Henry pronounced his fervid peroration, "Give me liberty or give me death," some five generations removed from the first Englishmen who had settled Massachusetts Bay and Virginia. They were a homogeneous people, all in all like-minded, inevitably self-conscious, regard-

[1] Cf. Barrett Wendell: *Liberty, Union and Democracy.* Scribner's.

ful of their roots in the mother country, and
speaking of her, even after the signing of the
Declaration of Independence, as "home." Some
of them, among the most cultivated and sensitive,
never succeeded in thinking of her as otherwise,
and, when the Revolution was effectuated, clung
to their allegiance and returned to England.
They preferred Union to Liberty, with regard
to the one commonwealth with which union was
natural, consanguineous as well as political.
Those who stayed preferred Liberty to Union,
and expressed their preference in a general formula which has become the point of departure
for all study of American ideals and American
practice. This formula is contained in the Declaration of Independence. It declares that all
men are created equal and "are endowed by the
Creator with certain unalienable rights," among
them being "life, liberty, and the pursuit of happiness." It declares government or political organization to be an instrument or tool to safe-
guard those rights, an instrument deriving its
"just powers from the consent of the governed."
And since—for the purposes of rebellion, at least
—the government of Great Britain had exceeded
its just powers and tried to exercise them in
America without "the consent of the governed"
the Declaration declared that "these United
Colonies are and of right ought to be free and

independent States"; that as such "they have full power to levy war, conclude peace, contract alliances, establish commerce, and to do all other acts and things which independent States may of right do."

The crux of this conception of Liberty lies in its fundamental implications that government is a tool, that its powers rest in the consent of the governed and that its function is to secure to the governed the definite original qualities inalienable from human existence. The ideal of Liberty which motivates the Revolution is a political and local, not a spiritual thing. It defines a reaction against conditions felt at the time to be oppressive, and unites, for the sole purpose of abolishing these conditions, thirteen sovereign and independent states. It does not regard their internal organization. It does not regard the facts of slavery and peonage. It does not regard the existence of class distinctions. It regards only the outer relations between England and her colonies, and it regards those solely in terms of economico-political, not social, cultural or religious organization. The sovereignty it aimed at, when declaring independence, was not the collective sovereignty of a United States; it was the distributive sovereignty of each state. The unit of Liberty was the separate colony, practically independent of the others and voluntarily allying

itself with the others for the achievement of a
common purpose. This alliance might or might
not continue after the purpose was achieved. It
was secondary, not primary. This fact is significant. It is preserved in the very name which the
country bears. The "United States of America"
contains no ethnic implication. Like the "United
Kingdom of Great Britain and Ireland," it designates a union of states, not a consanguineous
nationality. Germany, Russia, England, Denmark, France, any European country you will,
gets its name from a people who inhabit it. Its
nationality is a thing spontaneous and natural
rather than voluntary, rooted in hereditary
groupings far more than in reason and involving
consequently that self-centeredness which is characteristic of primary group life. The United
States, on the other hand, has a peculiar anonymity, and an anonymity which I like to think, in
my extremely hopeful and unreflective moods, is
formulated in the phrase that the American government is a government of laws, not men. This
anonymity is an effect of a conscious application
of a principle to an existing situation. It involves foresight and reason very much more than
"herd-instinct" and feeling. The American constitution is not a growth but an artifact, and
Americans have consequently a consciousness of
government and political responsibility which is

at the same time both freer and more intense
than anywhere else: they make more laws and respect fewer than any other people in the world.
During the period of the nation's nativity, men
knew that they were making a new start and ini-
tiating a novel practice. The fact that Thomas
Paine's *Common Sense* sold in thousands of
thousands of copies evidences this. It was in
Common Sense that he wrote: "We have it in our
power to begin the world over again. A situation
similar to the present hath not happened since
the days of Noah. The birthday of a new world
is at hand." This is the statement of a sober
thinker in a new environment, steeped in its practical problems and devoted to the making and
realization of its ideals. The new forms were,
however, none the less a continuance of the old
tradition. For a long time the question whether
the states were to remain separate or to be integrated into a union was such the decision of
which no one could foresee. What, in the conflict
of the ideal of Union with the ideal of local Liberty, finally decided it was not an ideal, but a
war prevailingly motivated by the conception of a
different type of Liberty.

This war, the great American Civil War,
solved by force the contradiction between Liberty
and Union. It abolished, perhaps not forever, the
conception of Liberty as local, and significantly,

it abolished this conception not wholly in the
name of Union, but wholly in the name of Liberty, specifying this ideal in a different direction;
namely, in the direction of Liberty of person
as against Liberty of organization. The meaning of liberty changed its character, and this
change was itself effected by the development of
a rival ideal—the ideal of Union.

The ideal of Union is in the order of time much
later than the older ideal of Liberty. It belongs
to the adolescence of the United States, and it
was involved in an economic conflict between two
regions: one, agrarian, where the landlord and
freeholder, owning slaves and practically self-
supporting, conserved the revolutionary tradition of the independence of statehood; the other,
progressively industrial and commercial, where
the growing economic interdependence led to the
conception of subordination of political rights to
changing economic needs, and consequently to a
constant encouragement of central authority over
local autonomy. The movement toward Union
was of such a fundamental nature that even Liberty's most ardent devotees and agitators, when
put in responsible positions, were bound to re-
enforce it. Thus, it was Thomas Jefferson who
consummated the Louisiana Purchase; it was
Andrew Jackson who destroyed nullification.

The whole history of the United States, prior

to the Civil War, is the history of conflict of the
ideals of Liberty, thought of locally, and Union,
thought of as the centralization of executive
power. Throughout the period the problem was
thought of and argued in terms political, although
its roots were profoundly economic. The hope of
the real devotees to America, hence the conception of Americanism, was the conservation and
reconciliation of both these ideals. It was
summed up in the conclusion to Webster's famous
reply to Hayne: "Liberty *and* Union, now and
forever, one and inseparable." Union came finally, after Webster died, at the end of a bitter
and galling war. It became in Lincoln's day far
more important than Liberty, as its danger at the
hands of the advocates of "state rights" grew
greater. To preserve the Union became Lincoln's fundamental and primary objective, and
the Civil War as he fought it was fought not to
free the slaves, but to maintain the unity of the
United States, toward which the liberation of the
slaves was an incidental contribution.

The possibility of conflict between central authority and local government is still present.
The unravelling of the complications between
California and Japan may carry still further the
process of unification or may arrest it *in statu
quo.* Mr. Roosevelt's *New Nationalism* has been
the latest authoritative utterance by an active and

influential politician on the one side of this question, and Mr. Wilson's *New Freedom,* by implication, on the other. In fact, however, the political hyphenation of state and nation is practically
abolished in both programs, and it is, all in all,
not undesirable that this abolition should be consummated if in this way real democracy can be
attained. The consummation is, of course, not
logical. In the struggle between Liberty and
Union the logic of the position was always on the
side of libertarians like Calhoun. Economic
facts, not political rhetoric, are the causal nexus
in the effectuation of events. These facts are expressed in the mood of the citizen, to whom the
unity of the country is now a politically accomplished fact. One no more spontaneously questions it than one questions the unity of a human
individual. Its accomplishment has shifted the
stress on the ideal of Liberty from locality to
person. In fact, Unionism would of itself never
have won in the Civil War because it would never
have obtained the adherents for war if it had not
been overwhelmingly reënforced by a new species
of libertarianism, that of Liberty of person, with
all the implications springing from the shifted incidence of the ideal. That is, the ideal of Union,
in changing from a sentiment to a fact, gained its
spiritual force in terms of the ideal of Democracy, and Democracy is the last element in the

trinity of Americanism to emerge. It is this ideal
which to-day holds the attention of most of
American politicians, statesmen, and the thoughtful classes. Whatever one may think of the
economic motivation of the struggle between the
North and the South, so much is certain: Without the great wave of humanitarian fervor which
sprang from New England transcendentalism
and of which Garrison was the loudest voice, a
fervor as unselfish and disinterested as any in
history, the fate of the Union might have been
otherwise. As it was, the conception of Union
was carried by the conception of personal Liberty. The aspiration of Webster would, in fact,
have been attained if the conception of Liberty
which came when Union was accomplished had
become a realized fact. It was, in intention, at
least, a much deeper Liberty, a much more distributive Liberty than the local Liberty which
opposed Union.

It is this distributive Liberty which is the essential in the ideal of Democracy. It began by
declaring the seat of consent of the governed to be
each human male individual who elects citizenship
in the country. It has now broadened the seat by
including the females. It causes the central government to owe its ultimate responsibility not to
the state, but to the individual. It points to all
other implications of democratic control which

are so much in the mouths of serious citizens and
interested politicians. It has involved Americans, of course, in any amount of confusion of
mind and in difficulties of situation. It has sub-
stituted government by indifference for government by consent of the governed, and has brought
into existence the economic and social mess which
has no possible justification in a country where
men have learned to think in national terms. The
indefiniteness of outlook which came with Union
meant to a large extent the failing of the civil
conscience which consciousness of fellowship in
the smaller state-group enforced. It threw men
too much back on themselves, made them *mere*
units, and this desocialization was emphasized by
the post-bellum rise of economic adventure, the
making of too great fortunes by too unscrupu-
lous means, and so on. It has rendered possible
government by election, i. e., by the untaught and
unreflective grace of majority suffrage rather
than government by fitness. It has led to the exploitation of class by class, of immigrant by native. It has led to the identification of economic
with ethnic differences. It has, in a word, created all the difficulties which people who think
merely in political terms try to remedy by further elaboration of political devices and multiplication of legislative instruments. It has, on the
other hand, acknowledged in men, by its inevita-

ble formulations, the full worth, and sometimes
even more than the full worth, of their manhood,
and has assumed, with a pathetic mystical optimism, the existence in each individual of a general human capacity which makes one man interchangeable for another, after the analogy of
mathematical units or parts in a machine.

The problems of Democracy, therefore, are
to-day the pressing problems, and under the new
conditions of life, conditions of which the Fathers
could have had no inkling, and for which they
certainly had no intention to provide, they re-
open on a new level the older questions, and re-
formulate the old ideals with a new meaning.

To-day the United States is one; more or less,
in Lincoln's phrase, "a government of the people,
by the people, for the people," whether good
or ill, and mitigated only by privileged economic
controls; a democracy in which the consent of the
governed is the ultimate basis for governmental
action, even though that basis gets rarely referred
to; and "life, liberty, and the pursuit of happiness" remain in a way and after a fashion its
goal. The American people, however, are no
longer one in the same sense in which the people
of Germany or the people of France are one, or
in which the people of the American Revolution were one. They are a mosaic of peoples, of different bloods and of different ori-

gins, engaged in rather different economic
fields, and varied in background and outlook as well as in blood. The ideal of Union no
longer involves that simplicity of organization
which is natural to an artificial form. The ideal
of Liberty is no longer rooted in the like-mindedness of a local group. The very conception of the
individual himself has changed. He is seen no
longer as an absolute distinct and autonomous
entity, but as a link in an endless historic chain
which is heredity, and as a point in a geographical extent involving political, economic, social organization, and all the other factors of group life,
which are his environment. American political
integrity is assured. American citizenship is no
more than citizenship in any land with free institutions: it is not a thing which fellow-countrymen
are born into, and from which they cannot escape,
so much as a thing which they choose and acquire
even when autochthonous, and which they can
give up when they find it incompatible with their
other ideals. The theory on which this action is
possible and allowed, a theory nowhere else actually applied, is the assertion of the Declaration of
Independence that government is a tool, not a
goal, that citizenship is voluntary, and that consequently it carries with it obligations as well as
privileges. No one resented the action of the late
Mr. Henry James when he found himself in such

disagreement with the attitude of the government of his country toward the European phase of the Great War that he could in conscience no longer retain his citizenship in it and gave it up. On the contrary, excuses and justifications were added to those he gave himself. His action means, of course, that citizenship is something based on free assent. To choose it is to declare it better than the type of citizenship abandoned in its favor. It means a consciousness of its character and the obligations it imposes as well as the privileges that it brings. It means not status, but a conscious contract. This of necessity should involve a higher degree of civic sense and civic responsibility than the citizenship which accrues as an accidental effect of nativity. That it does not do so in many instances, is a fact that requires a good deal of analysis. But that, other things being equal, it should and does do so seems to me indubitable, and it puts the problem of the status of the citizen in relation to the ideals of Liberty, Union, and Democracy in a new light. For each man or woman is the intersection of a line of ancestry and a line of social and cultural patterns and institutions, and it is what we are by heredity and early family influence that comes nearest to being inalienable and unalterable. The forms of our life, its flowering and fruitage, the things of the spirit, the character of happiness, whatever constitutes the goal of living, gets its quality and significance from these; they seem to be to the residue what the timbre of an instrument is to the tune played upon it. The residue, on the other hand, the economic and political organization of life, get their quality and significance from the materials used, and the abundance of living that they assure or permit. The latter is fundamental, but it appears to exist for the sake of the former only. A life of labor uncrowned with the spirit is an animal's life. And the problem of Democracy is so to perfect the organization of society that every man and every group may have the freest possible opportunity to realize and perfect their natures, and to attain the excellence appropriate to their kind. In essence, therefore, Democracy involves, not the elimination of differences, but the perfection and conservation of differences. It aims, through Union, not at uniformity, but at variety, at a one out of many, as the dollars say in Latin, and a many in one. It involves a give and take between radically different types, and a mutual respect and mutual coöperation based on mutual understanding. It is this ideal which to my mind seems most naturally the proper content of the interplay of the terms Liberty and Union and Democracy. The older political-economic significances of those terms should by now have become the indispensable foundations of others. They should have entered the implicit, funded consciousness of the country. Without them no freedom of the spirit is possible, and no creative culture.

To-day, however, the issue of democracy has taken on a vexatious character. The civil war in Europe has indicated that the natural hyphenation of the American citizen may become the basis for disruptive action, and as a consequence, the term "hyphenated American" has become a term of reproach. That is as it may be. In time of danger, passions run high, no thought is taken as a preliminary to action, and analysis is replaced by denunciation. Clearly, any citizen of the United States who in his country or out of it uses his citizenship to the disadvantage of his own country for the sake of an enemy is properly called traitor, and deserves to be treated as such. He is all the more a traitor because his citizenship is voluntary, and could not be forced upon him against his will. Under the law, too often violated during the draft, the country exercises no claim upon him, if he chooses not to exercise a claim upon it. Such disloyalty is, however, a very different thing from natural hyphenation.

Hyphenation as such is a fact which permeates all levels of life. A man is at once a son and a husband, a brother and a friend, a man of affairs and a student, a citizen of a state and a member

of a church, one in an ethnic and social group
and the citizen of a nation. It is obvious that any
one of these relationships may tend to outweigh
any of the others, and may give rise to divided
and sometimes radically antagonistic allegiances.
But it is absurd to lose sight of the truth that the
hyphen unites very much more than it separates,
and that in point of fact, the greater the hyphenation, the greater the unanimity. There are, actual
and implicit, in the very principle of organization
of the American republic, factions of political
hyphenation in the conflict between state and
national interests as those became manifest from
time to time. There is ethnic hyphenation in the
differences of race, origin, and character among
the various peoples who constitute the American
citizenry. In the case of the negro, the hyphenation is insisted on, and it is doubtful whether even
the late Mr. Roosevelt could have brought himself to consent to a son of his marrying a negress.
There is the customary and practically certain
danger of what William James used to call "vicious abstractionism" in the legislative and popular dealing with the hyphen, and it is necessary
to specify and to specify definitely just what kind
of hyphenation is likely to be a public menace
and when, and how, and just what kind helps to-
wards the bringing into existence of the Americanism designated in the progression of Liberty,

Union, and Democracy. The union which the
hyphen designates is the new content of the ancestral ideal of Union, and it lies in the background of the national history of the United
States. In the individual, this union is what we
designate by culture, and culture is nothing more
than spiritual hyphenation—it is humanism in the
best sense of the term. For the essential of humanism is sympathetic recognition and understanding of differences in outlook, differences in
origin, differences in nature, and conservation of
and coöperation with those differences. In education, at least, nationalism means invariably
limits, and consequently stagnation and slow
death. One need only think of the Chinese. The
cultivated man, whether he be an Englishman or
a German, is essentially a citizen of the world because from his firm seat in his own home, he
understands and coöperates with spiritual expressions having a different base, a different background, and a different import from his own for
the spirit of man.

In a certain sense, Americanism as a social
ideal could be identified with the ideal of culture.
To be a citizen of the United States would then
be the same in value as being a citizen of the
world. Here, on the North American continent,
because of the postulations in Liberty, Union,
and Democracy, made by the Fathers, people of

all origins and of different gifts can and often do live and labor together in amity and coöperation in the building of a great free commonwealth which shall secure life, liberty and happiness to each individual and each group concerned in the enterprise. Its principle tends willy-nilly, even if laggingly, to be the principle of all for one and one for all; as Webster said it, "Liberty and Union, now and forever, one and inseparable."

The emphatic teaching of the implications of this principle for the development of the history of the country seems to me the most important nearest task for those who are concerned about the country's future. What with the welter of the vocational interests and pedagogic fads, the insatiable greed of the industrial machine, that which has sometimes been called the Great Vocation is forgotten. This vocation is citizenship. In a democracy it is fundamental, for a democracy dares to endow each citizen with the task that Plato, who was so wise in his own democratic generation, left to a hardily trained and expert few. It assumes that each citizen, with all his allegiances and other imperfections on his head, is to be the guardian of the State, and that the State is to secure him freedom and safety in his endeavors, his achievements, and his associations. The basis of the guardianship, hence, can, to give any promise of its proper discharge, be hardly less

than a vision of the whole complex and hyphenation of American society, in all its forms; and
nothing less in the teaching of the native-born or
immigrant is adequate to keep Americans what,
in spite of many tragic shortcomings and difficulties, in spite of much disillusion and some despair,
still has the distinction of having been, as Paine
thought, a beginning of the world over again, an
experiment in social justice, rooted in a living
faith in the potential excellence of every man, and
every natural group, according to kind: a faith in
the power and will of men to realize service
through freedom, and freedom through service.
The latter end, one must concede to the critics of
American civilization, seems very contrary to the
beginning.   Is it, however, written in the stars
that it need remain so?

II

DEMOCRACY *VERSUS* THE
MELTING-POT[1]

I

IT was, I think, an eminent lawyer who, backed
by a ripe experience of inequalities before the
law, pronounced the American Declaration of
Independence to be a collection of "glittering
generalities." Yet it cannot be that the implied
slur was deserved. There is hardly room to
doubt that the equally eminent gentlemen over
whose signatures this orotund synthesis of the social and political philosophy of the 18th century
appears conceived that they were subscribing to
anything but the dull and sober truth when they
underwrote the doctrine that God had created
all men equal and had endowed them with certain inalienable rights, among these being life,
liberty, and the pursuit of happiness. That this
doctrine did not describe a condition, that it even
contradicted conditions, that many of the signa-

[1] Printed in *The Nation*. February 18 and 25, 1915.

tories owned other men and bought and sold them, that many were eminent by birth, many by wealth and only a few by merit—all this is acknowledged. Indeed, they were aware of these inequalities; they would probably have fought against their abolition. But they did not regard them as incompatible with the Declaration of Independence. For to them the Declaration was neither a pronouncement of abstract principles nor an exercise in formal logic. It was an instrument in a political and economic conflict, a weapon of offense and defense. The doctrine of "natural rights" which is its essence was formulated to shield social orders against the aggrandizement of persons acting under the doctrine of "divine right": its function was to afford sanction for refusing customary obedience to traditional superiority. Such also was the function of the Declaration. Across the water, in England, certain powers had laid claim to the acknowledgment of their traditional superiority to the colonists in America. Whereupon the colonists, through their representatives, the signatories to the Declaration, replied that they were quite as good as their traditional betters, and that no one should take from them certain possessions which were theirs. This is the whole, actual, historic meaning of the Declaration of Independence: this is what it expressed as an *action*—resistance to the aggrandizement of a traditionally superior force. Formulas are, however, much more indefinite than actions, for if deeds speak louder than words, words last longer and spread farther. Hence, what has survived of the Declaration in the imagination of Americans is not its practical meaning; what has survived is its verbal and logical meaning. And hence, again, a paradox—

To-day the descendants of the colonists appear to be reformulating a Declaration of Independence. Again, as in 1776, Americans of British ancestry apprehend that certain possessions of theirs, which may be lumped under the word "Americanism" are in jeopardy. The danger comes, once more, from a force across the water, but the force is this time regarded not as superior, but as inferior. The relationships of 1776 are, consequently, reversed. To conserve the inalienable rights of the colonists of 1776, it was necessary to declare all men equal; to conserve the inalienable rights of their descendants in the 20th century, it becomes necessary to declare all men unequal. In 1776 all men were as good as their betters; in 1920 men are permanently worse than their betters. "A nation may reason," writes one nervous professor, in embattled defense,[1] " 'Why burden ourselves with the rearing of children?

[1] E. A. Ross in *The Old World in the New.*

Let them perish unborn in the womb of time. The immigrants will keep up the population.' A people that has no more respect for its ancestors and no more pride of race than this deserves the extinction that surely awaits it."

Respect for ancestors, pride of race! Time was when these would have been repudiated as the enemies of democracy, the antithesis of the fundamentals of the North American Republic, with its consciously proclaimed belief that "a man's a man for a' that." And now they are being invoked in defense of democracy, against the "melting-pot," by a sociological protagonist of the "democratic idea." How knowingly purposeful their invocation is cannot be said. But that its assumptions have unconsciously colored much of the social and political thinking of the United States from the days of the Cincinnati on, seems to me unquestionable, and it seems even more unquestionable that this apparently sudden and explicit conscious expression of them is the effect of an actual felt menace. This professor, in a word, is no voice crying in a wilderness. He simply utters aloud, and in his own peculiar manner, what is thought and spoken wherever Americans of British ancestry congregate feelingly. His sentiment utters the more recent phase of the operation of these forces in the social and economic history of the United States; he is, in effect, a voice and instrument of theirs. Being so, he could, of course, neither take account of them nor observe them; he could only react in terms of them to the processes of American society that seem to threaten the supremacy of his stock and caste. The reaction is secondary, the threat is secondary. The standards alone are really primary and, perhaps, ultimate. Fully to understand the place and function of "the old world in the new," and the attitude of the "new world" toward the old, demands an appreciation of the influence of these primary and ultimate standards upon all the peoples who are citizens of the country.

II

In 1776 the mass of white men in the colonies *were* actually, with respect to each other, rather free and rather equal. I refer, not so much to the absence of great differences in wealth, as to the fact that the whites were prevailingly *like-minded*. They were possessed of ethnic and cultural unity; they were homogeneous with respect to ancestry and ideals. Their century-and-a-half-old tradition as Americans was continuous with their immemorially older traditions as Britons. They did not, until the economico-political quarrel with the mother country arose, regard themselves as other than Englishmen, sharing England's dangers and England's glories. When the quarrel came they remembered how they had left the mother country in search of religious liberty for themselves, how they had left Holland, where they had found this liberty, for fear of losing their ethnic and cultural identity, and what hardships they bore for the sake of conserving both the liberty and the identity. Upon these they grafted that political liberty, the love of which was, as the veracious history books tell us, no doubt inborn, but the expression of which was occasioned by the competition of colonial merchants with the merchants of England. This grafting was not, of course, conscious. The continuity established itself rather as a mood than as an articulate idea. The economic situation was only an occasion and not a cause. The cause lay in the homogeneity of the people, in their *like-mindedness,* and in their *self-consciousness.* From the settlement of Plymouth to the signing of the Declaration the British colonists in America were conscious of an individuality, of definite common ideals and purposes and heritage which they sought to realize and to aggrandize.

Now it would seem that the preservation, though not the development, of any given type of civilization rests very largely upon these two conditions—like-mindedness and self-consciousness. Without them art, literature, culture in any of its nobler forms, appear to be unlikely: and colonial America had a culture—chiefly of New England—but representative enough of the whole British-American life of the period. Within the area of what we now call the United States this life was not, however, the only life. Similarly animated groups of Frenchmen and Germans in Louisiana and Pennsylvania regarded themselves as the cultural peers of the British, and because of their own common ancestry, their own like-mindedness and self-consciousness, they have retained a large measure of their individuality and spiritual autonomy to this day, after generations of unrestricted and mobile contact and a century of political union with the dominant British populations.

In the course of time the state which began to be with the Declaration of Independence became possessed of all the continental area known as the United States. French and Germans in Louisiana and Pennsylvania remained at home; the descendants of the British colonists trekked across the continent, leaving tiny self-conscious nuclei of population in their wake, and so established ethnic and cultural standards for the whole country. Had the increase of these settlements borne the same proportion to the unit of population that it bore between 1810 and 1820, the Americans of British stock would have numbered

to-day over 100 millions. The inhabitants of the
country do number over 100 millions; but they
are not the children of the colonists and pioneers:
they are later immigrants and the children of
later immigrants, and they are not British merely
but of all the other European stocks.

First came the Irish, integral to the polity of
Great Britain but ethnically different, Catholic
in religion, fleeing from economic and political
oppression, and, therefore, self-conscious and rebellious. They came seeking food and freedom,
and revenge against the oppressors on the other
side. Their area of settlement is chiefly the East.
There they were not met with open arms. Historically only semi-alien, their appearance
aroused, none the less, both fear and active op-
positions. Their diversity in religion was so conspicuous, their gregarious politics so disturbing.
Opposition, economic, religious, political and social, by organizing, stimulated their natural gre-
gariousness to militancy. They formed associations in their turn, religious and political. Slowly
they made their way, slowly they came to power,
establishing themselves in many modes as potent
—every one knows how potent—forces in the life
of America. Many Americans hold that they
have their virtue still to prove; how, they do not
care to say. To the dispassionate observer with-

out ethnic bias, they constitute an approved ethnic unit of the white American population.

Behind the Irish came the great mass of the Germans, quite diverse in speech and customs, culturally and economically far better off than the Irish, and self-conscious, as well through oppression and political aspiration as for these other reasons. They settled inland, over a stretch of relatively continuous territory extending from western New York to the Mississippi—from Buffalo to Minneapolis, and from Minneapolis to St. Louis. Spiritually these Germans were more akin to the American settlers than the Irish, and indeed, although social misprision received them also, they were less coldly accepted and with less difficulty tolerated. As they made their way, greater and greater numbers of the peasant stock joined them in the western nuclei of population, so that between the Great Lakes and Mississippi Valley they constitute the prevailing ethnic type.

Beyond them, in Minnesota and the Dakotas and thereabout, their near neighbors, the Scandinavians, prevail, and beyond these, in the mountain and mining regions, the central and eastern and southern Europeans—Slavs of various stocks, Magyars, Finns, Italians. Across the Rockies, cut off from the rest of the country by this natural barrier, a stratum of Americans of

British ancestry balances the thinnish stratum on
the Atlantic sea-coast; flanked on the south by
Latins—Spanish, Mexican, Italian—and scat-
tering groups of Asiatics, and on the north by
Scandinavians. The distribution of the population upon the two coasts is not dissimilar; that
upon the Atlantic littoral is only less homogeneous. There French-Canadians, Irish, Italians,
Slavs and Jews alternate with the British-American population and each other, while in the West
the "Americans" lie between and surround the
Italians, Asiatics and Scandinavians.

Of all these "immigrant" peoples the greater
part were of peasant stock, vastly illiterate, living
their lives at fighting weight, with a minimum of
food and a maximum of toil. The fearful Americans think that their coming to the United States
was determined by no spiritual urge; only the
urge of steamship agencies and economic need or
greed. However generally plausible this opinion
may be, it ignores, curiously enough, four significant, and one notable, exceptions to it. The significant exceptions are the Poles, the Finns, the
Bohemians, the Slovaks—the only recently subject Slavic nationalities generally. Political and
religious and cultural persecution plays no small
rôle in the movement of the masses of them. The
notable exception is the Jews. The Jews come
far more with the attitude of the vaunted earliest

settlers than any of the other peoples; for they more than any other present-day immigrant group are in flight from persecution and disaster; in search of economic opportunity, liberty of conscience, civil rights. They have settled chiefly in the northeast, with New York City as the center of greatest concentration. Among them, as among the Puritans, the Pennsylvania Germans, the French of Louisiana, self-consciousness and like-mindedness have been intense and articulate. But they differ from the lately subjugated Slavic peoples in that the latter look backward and forward to *actual,* even if enslaved homelands; the Jews in the mass have thus far looked to America as their homeland, and seem, with all their Zionism, likely to continue to do so.

In sum, when we consider that portion of our population which has taken root, we see that it has not merely stippled the country in small units of diverse ethnic groups. It forms rather a series of stripes or layers of varying sizes, moving east to west along the central axis of settlement, where towns are thickest; i. e., from New York and Philadelphia through Chicago and St. Louis, to San Francisco and Seattle. Stippling does not prevail even in the towns, where the variety of population is generally greater. Probably more than half of that population is either foreign-born or of non-British stock, yet even so, the towns are aggregations, not units. Broadly divided into the sections inhabited by the rich and those inhabited by the poor, this economic division does not abolish, it only crosses, the ethnic one. There are rich and poor little Italys, Irelands, Hungarys, Germanys, and rich and poor Ghettos. The *common* city-life, which depends upon like-mindedness, is not inward, corporate and inevitable, but external, inarticulate and incidental, a reaction to the need of amusement and the need of protection, not the expression of a homogeneity of heritage, mentality and interest. Politics and education in our cities thus often present the phenomenon of ethnic compromises not unknown in the former Austria-Hungary: concessions and appeals to "the Irish vote," "the Jewish vote," "the German vote" vary with concessions and appeals to "the business vote," "the labor vote," and "the woman vote"; occasionally there are compromise school-committees whose members represent each ethnic faction, until, as in Boston, one group grows strong enough to dominate the entire situation.

South of Mason and Dixon's line the cities exhibit a greater homogeneity. Outside of certain regions in Texas the descendants of the native white stock, often degenerate and backward, prevail among the whites, but the whites as a whole constitute a relatively weaker proportion of

the population. They live among nine million negroes, whose own mode of living tends, by its
mere massiveness, to standardize the "mind" of
the poor white, of the proletarian south, in speech,
manner and the other values of social living, and
to determine the terrible pattern which, among
other things, the fear of negro competition makes
race-prejudice take.

III

All immigrants and their offspring are by the
way of undergoing "Americanization" if they remain in one place in the country long enough—
say six or seven years. The general notion of
"Americanization" appears to signify the adoption of the American variety of English speech,
American clothes and manners, the American attitude in politics. "Americanization" signifies, in
short, the disappearance of the external differences upon which so much race-prejudice often
feeds. It appears to imply the fusion of the
various bloods, and a transmutation by "the
miracle of assimilation" of Jews, Slavs, Poles,
Frenchmen, Germans, Hindus, Scandinavians
and so on into beings similar in background,
tradition, outlook and spirit to the descendants
of the British colonists, the "Anglo-Saxon"
stock. Broadly speaking, these elements of

Americanism are somewhat external, the effect of environment; largely internal, the effect of heredity, social and personal. Thus American economic individualism, American traditional *laissez-faire* policy is largely the effect of environment; where nature offers more than enough potential wealth to go round, there is no immediate need for regulating distribution. What poverty and unemployment exist in the United States are the result of unskilled and wasteful social housekeeping, not of any actual natural barrenness. And until the disparity between the economic resources and the population of the United States becomes equalized, so that the country will attain an approximate economic equilibrium, this is likely to continue to be the case. With American individualism go American optimism, and the other "pioneer" virtues—they are purely reactions to the country's unexploited natural wealth, and as such are moods which characterize all societies where the relation between population and resource is similar. The curious alternation of Professor Wilson's "new freedom" with Colonel Roosevelt's "new nationalism" is the most illuminating expression of this relationship in the political mode, and the overwhelming concern of both newnesses with the economic situation rather than with the cultural or spiritual is a still better one. That the latter alone justify or condemn this or that economic condition or program is a commonplace: by their fruits shall ye know the soil and the roots.

The fruits in this case have been mostly those of New England. Eliminate from the American roster of the cultural era now being forgotten— Whittier, Longfellow, Lowell, Hawthorne, Emerson, Howells—and who are left? Outstanding are Poe and Whitman, and the neo-romantic mysticism of the former is only a sick-minded version of the naturalistic mysticism of the latter, while the general mood of both is that of Emerson, who in his way expresses the culmination of that movement in mysticism from the agonized conscience of colonial and Puritan New England—to which Hawthorne gives voice—to the serene and optimistic assurance which is the tone of Emerson. In religion this spirit of Puritan New England non-conformity culminates similarly, in Christian Science when it is superstitious and magical, in Unitarianism when it is rationalistic. In both cases, over against the personal individualism of the economic and political scene there is set the cosmic unity of the heavenly mansions. For New England, religious, political and literary interests remained coördinate and undivided; and New England gave the tone to and established the standards for the rest of American society. Save for the very early aristocratic

political writers defending democracy, the "solid
South" remains illiterate and unexpressed, while
the march of the pioneer across the continent is
permanently marked by Mark Twain for the
Middle West, and by Bret Harte for the Pacific
slope. Both these men carry something of the
time and spirit of New England—less of its ultimate serenity and more of its first agony perhaps
—and with them the "great tradition" of America, the America of the "Anglo-Saxon," finds its
phase. There remains nothing large or significant of that old order and vanished life that is unexpressed, and no unmentioned writer who is so
completely representative.

The background, tradition, temper and outlook of the whole of the America of the "Anglo-
Saxon," then, find their spiritual and contempo-
raneous expression in the New England School,
Poe, Whitman, Mark Twain, Bret Harte. They
realize an individual who has passed from the
agonized to the optimistic conscience, a person of
the solid and homely virtues tempered by mystic
certainty of his destiny, his election, hence always
ready to take risks, and always willing to face
dangers. From the agony of Arthur Dimmes-
dale to the robustious industrial and social adventure of Silas Lapham, from the irresponsible
kindliness of Huck Finn to the *Luck of Roar-
ing Camp,* the movement is continuous, though

on different social levels. In regions supernal its coördinate is the movement from the God of Jonathan Edwards to the Oversoul of Emerson and the she-Divinity of Mary Eddy. It is summed up in the contemporary representative "average" American of British stock—an individualist, speaking an English dialect, interested in getting on, kind, neighborly, not too scrupulous in business, rather elemental in his pleasures, indulgent to his women, unthinkingly devoted to "laissez-faire" in economics and politics, very respectable in private life, tending to liberalism and mysticism in religion, naïvely credulous of the black arts and the sciences; moved, where his economic interests are unaffected, by formulas rather than ideas, in all matters by preference a "booster" rather than a "knocker." He typifies the aristocracy of America.[1] From among his fellows are recruited her foremost protagonists in politics, religion, art and learning. He regards himself, in virtue of being heir of the oldest *rooted* economic settlement and spiritual tradition of the white man in North America, the measure and the standard of the Americanism that the newcomer is to attain.

Other things being equal, a democratic society which was to be a realization of the assumptions

---

[1] Recently there has appeared a sociological novel, *Babbitt*, by Sinclair Lewis, which is a close, if somewhat external, study of the type.

of the Declaration of Independence, supposing them to be true and socially operative, would be a leveling society such that all persons in it became alike either on the lowest or the highest plane. The outcome of free social contacts should, according to "the laws of imitation," establish "equality" on the highest plane; for imitation is said to be of the higher by the lower, so that the cut of a Paris gown at $1,000.00 becomes imitated in department stores at $17.50, and the play of the rich becomes the vice of the poor. This process of leveling up through imitation is facilitated by the so-called "standardization" of externals. In these days of ready-made garments, factory-made furniture, refrigerating plants, "boiler-plate," movies and radio, it is almost impossible that the mass of the inhabitants of the United States should wear other than uniform clothes, use other than uniform furniture, utensils or eat anything but the same sorts of food, read anything but the same syndicated hokum, see anything but the same standardized romances and hear anything but the same broadcasted barbarisms. In these days of rapid transit and industrial mobility it must seem impossible that any stratification of population should be permanent. Hardly anybody seems to have been born where he lives, or to live where he has been born. The teetering of demand and supply in industry and commerce keep large masses of population constantly mobile: so that many people no longer can be said to have homes. This mobility reën-forces the need of the immigrant to learn English —for a *lingua franca* intelligible everywhere be-comes indispensable. And ideals that are felt to belong with the language tend to become "standardized," widespread, uniform, through the devices of the telegraph and the telephone, the syndication of "literature," the cheap news-paper and the cheap novel, the vaudeville circuit, the phonograph, the player piano, the movie, and the star-system and the radio. Even more signifi-cantly, mobility leads to the propinquity of the different 'stocks, thus promoting intermarriage and pointing to the coming of a new "American race"—a blend of at least all the European stocks (for some doubt is expressed even by the white population of the South as to whether negroes —of whom more than a third are already of mixed blood—should also constitute an element in this blend) into a newer and better being whose qualities and ideals shall be the qualities and ideals of the contemporary American of British ancestry. Apart from the unintentional im-pulsion of the conditions I have just enumerated toward this end, there exists in addition an instru-ment especially devised for this purpose. The instrument is called the public school. With it there may be reckoned to some extent the state institutions of higher education—normal schools and universities. That the end has been and is being attained, we have outstanding among many others the biographical testimony of such significant personalities as Jacob Riis and Edward Steiner and Mary Antin—a Dane and two Jews, intermarried, "assimilated" even in religion, and more excessively, self-consciously flatteringly American than the Americans. And another Jew, Mr. Israel Zangwill, of London, England, profitably promulgates this end as a principle and an aspiration, to the admiring approval of American audiences, under the device, "the melting-pot."

IV

All is not, however, fact, because it is hope; nor is the biography of an individual, particularly of a literary individual, the history of a group. The Riises and Steiners and Antins together with Edward Bok and their numerous other recent imitators mostly female and Jewish, protest too much; they are too self-conscious and self-centered, their "Americanization" appears too much like an achievement, a *tour de force,* too little like a growth. As for Zangwill—at best he is the obverse of Dickens, at worst he is a Jew making a special plea. It is the work of the

Americanized writers that is really significant, and in that one senses, underneath the excellent writing, a dualism, and the strain to overcome it. The same dualism is apparent in different form, among the "Americans," and the strain to overcome it seems even stronger. These appear to have been most explicit at the high-water marks of periods of immigration: the Know-Nothing Party was one early expression of it; another was the organization, in the '80's, of the patriotic societies—the Sons and the Daughters of the American Revolution, later on of the Colonial Dames and so on; there are scores of them. Since the Spanish War it has shown itself in the continual if uneven growth of the political conscience, first as a muck-raking magazine propaganda, then as a nationwide attack on the corruption of politics by plutocracy, finally as the altogether respectable and evangelical and futile and betrayed Progressive Party, with its slogan of "human rights against property rights." Coincidently, the literature of the muckrake has developed into the sociological novel, the road being natural from the investigations by Miss Ida Tarbell to the dramatizations of Mr. Frank Norris, Mr. Theodore Dreiser, Mr. Robert Herrick, Mr. Upton Sinclair. The new political program is synchronous with the showing-up of the "captain of industry," and the showing-up of the "captain of industry" is synchronous with the most massive waves of immigration.

In this process, however, the non-British American or continental immigrant has not been a fundamental protagonist. He has been an occasion rather than a force. What has been causal has been "American." Consider, by way of demonstration, the personnel and history of the Progressive Party: it was recruited largely from the professional groups and from the solid lower and upper middle class; there were more farmers than workers in it. As a spirit it had survived in Kansas, which by a historic accident happens to be the one middle-western state predominantly Yankee; as a victorious party it lived on for a time in California, one of the few states outstandingly "American" in population. What is significant in it, as in every other form in which the political conscience expresses itself, is the fact that it is a response to a feeling of "something out of gear," and naturally one's attention seeks the cause first of all outside of one's self, not within. Hence the interest in economico-political reconstruction. But the maladjustment in that region is really external. And the political conscience is seeking by a mere change in outward condition to abolish an inward disparity. "Human rights *versus* property rights" is merely the modern version of the Declaration of Independence, still assuming that

men are men merely, as like as marbles, and des-
tined under uniformity of conditions to uniformity of spirit. The course of American economic
history since the Civil War shows aptly enough
how shrewd were, other things being equal,
Marx's generalizations concerning the tendencies
of capital toward concentration in the hands of a
few. Attention consequently has fixed itself
more and more upon the equalization of the distribution of wealth—not socialistically, of course
not; in the spirit of true Americanism, undiluted
and 100 proof. And this will really abolish
the dualism if the economic bifurcation into
rich and poor should prove to be the more fundamental one. It happens, so far, that it doesn't
seem to be. The "Anglo-Saxon" American, con-
stituting as he does, the economic upper-class,
would hardly have reacted to economic disparity
as he has, if that had been the only disparity. In
point of fact it is the ethnic disparity, which has
reënforced the economic, that troubles him. His
activity as entrepreneur has crowded the cities of
his country with progressively cheaper laborers
of continental stock, all consecrated to the uses of
the industrial machine; and towns like Gary,
Lawrence, Chicago, Pittsburgh, Pawtucket,
have become gigantic camps of foreign industrial
mercenaries. His undertakings have brought
into being the efficient autocracies of the charac-

ter of Pullman, Illinois, or Lead, South Dakota. They have created a mass of casual laborers numbering in the vicinity of 5,000,000 and of work-children to the number of approximately 1,500,-000 (the latter chiefly in the South, where the purely "American" white more than predominates and southern chivalry is sucked with the mother's milk). They have done all this because economic law—only foreign envy would call it the greed of the entrepreneur—has displaced high-demanding labor by cheaper labor, and has brought into being the unnecessary problem of unemployment. In all things this economic law —let us never commit the foreign heresy of calling it greed—has set the standard, so that the working ideal of the people is to get rich, to live and to think as the rich, to subordinate government to the service of wealth, making the actual government "invisible." What else could the "price-system" allow them to hope for? If there exist "labor unrest," false economic doctrine like socialism and such, civil wars such as those in Colorado, in West Virginia, in Oregon, in Massachusetts, how can these be due to the beneficent providence of economic law and not to foreign viciousness and "trouble-makers"?

Because the great mass of the laborers happen to be of continental and not of British ancestry, and because they are late comers, the guilt for this perversion of American public life and social ideals must, of course, accrue to them. There can be only eugenic perfection and political wisdom in the degenerate farming stock of New England, the "poor whites" of the South, the negroes. The anthropological as well as the economic menace to the 100 per cent integrity of the American can come only from the "fusion" of these continental Europeans—Slavs, and Italians and Jews—with the native stock. Professors of sociology, if their race is right, must properly grow anxious over the fate of American institutions in such hands. Take such a work, for example, as E. A. Ross's *The Old World in the New.* Nothing could better illustrate the fact that the dualism is as inevitably ethnic as it is economic. Under the "laissez-faire" policy the economic process would have been the same, of whatever race the rich, and whatever race the poor. Only race prejudice, primitive, spontaneous and unconscious, could have caused a trained economist to ignore the so obvious fact that in a capitalistic industrial society labor is useless and helpless without capital; that hence the external dangers of immigration are in the greed of the capitalist and the indifference of the government. The proper restriction of immigration can naturally succeed only with the restriction of the entrepreneur's greed, which is its cause,

and the abolition of his control on government
by which he works his effects. But the abolition
of immigration and the restoration of the supremacy of "human rights" over "property
rights" need not abolish the fundamental ethnic
dualism, and may aggravate it.

The reason is obvious. That like-mindedness
in virtue of which men are as nearly as is possible
in fact "free and equal" is not primarily the result of a constant set of external conditions. Its
prepotent cause is a prevailing intrinsic similarity, which, for the United States, has its roots in
that ethnic and cultural unity of which American
fundamental institutions are declared to be the
most durable expression. Similar environments,
similar occupations, do, of course, generate similarities. "American" is an adjective of similarity
applied to English, Welsh, Scotch, Irish, Jews,
Germans, Italians, Poles and so on. But the
similarity is one of place and institution; acquired, not inherited, and hence not inevitably
transmitted. Each generation has, in fact, to become "Americanized" afresh, and withal, inherited nature has a way of redirecting nurture of
which American public schools give extensive evidence. If the inhabitants of the United States
are stratified economically as "rich" and "poor,"
they are stratified ethnically as Germans, Scandinavians, Jews, Irish, and so on; and although the

two stratifications cross more frequently than they are coincident, they interfere with each other far less than is hopefully supposed. The history of the "International" prior to the Great War, the present *débâcle* in Europe are indications of how little "class-consciousness" modifies other types of consciousness, including consciousness of nationality and patriotism. To the dominant nationality in America "nationality" in the European sense used to have no meaning: for it had itself been the measure of the country's excellence, and had been assimilating others to itself. Now that the process seems to be slowed down, it thinks it finds itself confronted with the problem of nationality just as do the Irish, the Poles, the Bohemians, the Czechs and the other oppressed nationalities in Europe. "We are submerged," wrote a great American man of letters, who has better than any one else I know of interpreted to the world the spirit of America as New England, "we are submerged beneath a conquest so complete that the very name of us means something not ourselves. . . . I feel as I should think an Indian might feel, in the face of ourselves that were."

The fact is that similarity of class rests upon no inevitable external condition: while similarity of nationality has usually a considerable intrinsic base. Hence the poor of two different peoples tend to be less like-minded than the poor and the rich of the same peoples. At his core, no human being, even in a "state of nature," is a mere mathematical unit of action like the "economic man." Behind him in time and tremendously in him in quality, are his ancestors; around him in space are his relatives and kin, carrying in common with him the inherited organic set from a remoter common ancestry. In all these he lives and moves and has his being. They constitute his, literally, *natio,* the inwardness of his nativity, and in Europe every inch of his non-human environment wears the effects of their action upon it and breathes their spirit. The America he comes to, beside Europe, is Nature virgin and inviolate: it does not guide him with ancestral blazings: externally he is cut off from the past. Not so internally: whatever else he changes, he cannot change his grandfather. Moreover, he comes rarely alone; he comes companioned with his fellow nationals; and he comes to no strangers, but to kin and friends who have gone before. If he is able to excel, he soon achieves a local habitation. There he encounters the native American to whom he is merely a Dutchman, a Mick, a frog, a wop, a dago, a hunky, or a sheeny and no more; and he encounters these others who are unlike him, dealing with him as a lower and outlandish creature. Then, be he even the rudest and most

primeval peasant, heretofore totally unconscious
of his nationality, of his categorical difference
from many men and similarity to some, he must
inevitably become conscious of it. Thus, in the
industrial and congested towns of the United
States, where there are real and large contacts between immigrant nationalities, the first effect
appears to be an intensification of spiritual dissimilarities, always to the disadvantage of the
dissimilarities.

The second generation, consequently, devotes
itself feverishly to the attainment of similarity.
The social tradition of its parents is lost by attrition or thrown off for advantage. The merest
externals of the new one are acquired—via the
street and the public school. But as the public
school imparts it, or as the social settlement imparts it, it is not really a *life;* it is an abstraction,
an arrangement of words. America is a word:
as a historic fact, or as a democratic ideal of life,
it is not realized at all. At best and at worst—
now that the captains of industry are showing
disturbance over the mess they have made, and
"vocational training" is becoming a part of the
public educational program—the prospective
American learns a trade, acquiring at his most
impressionable age the habit of being a cog in the
industrial machine. And this he learns, moreover, from the sons and daughters of earlier im-

migrants, themselves essentially uneducated and nearly illiterate, with what spontaneity and teaching power they once owned squeezed out of them in the "normal" schools by the application of the Pecksniffian "efficiency"-press called pedagogy.

But *life,* the liberation of feeling and effectuation of purposes, the prospective American learns from the yellow press, the movies, and similar engines which have set themselves explicitly the task of appealing to his appetites. He learns of the wealth, the luxuries, the extravagances and the immoralities of specific rich persons. He learns to want to be like them. As that is impossible in the mass, their amusements become his crimes or vices. Or suppose him to be lucky enough or strong enough to emerge from the proletarian into the middle class, to win for himself economic security and social respectability. He remains still the Slav, the Jew, the German or the Irish citizen of the American state. Again, in the mass, neither he nor his children nor his children's children lose their ethnic individuality. True, there is intermarriage, often much of it. But on the whole and in the mass, marriage is determined by sexual selection and by propinquity, and the larger the homogeneous communities in any city, the less likely are mixed marriages to take place. Although the gross number of such marriages is considerably above what it was fifty years ago, the relative proportion in terms of variant units of population tends, I think, to be significantly less. As the stratification of the towns echoes and stresses the stratification of the country as a whole, the likelihood of a new "American" race is remote enough, and the fear of it unnecessary. But equally remote also is the possibility of a universalization of the inward bases of the old American life. Only the externals succeed in passing over.

The geographic extent of the country intensifies this remoteness. It takes the fastest train no less than four days—one could cross Europe in that time easily—to pass from New York to San Francisco, and almost two to pass from Chicago to New Orleans. Historic sectional differences between North and South, East and West, have emerged not only in economic and political matters but in manner and outlook. In the instance of the Civil War these differences became momentous. They still persist, and in addition each section, East, West, North and South, is peopled by white men of different European stocks and traditions. They add diversity to diversity, and when one speaks of their inward Americanization, one wonders also to just what local type this inward change must assimilate itself. There are, of course, the great labor gangs that move like mercenaries from place to place. But they are out of question when one speaks of "Americanization," for the adage about the rolling stone is notorious, and the moss we call culture, even the culture of America, requires a broad and quiet back to grow on, when the back is native. How, when the back is foreign?

It took up to two hundred years of settled life in one place for the New England School to emerge, and it emerged in a community in which like-mindedness was very strong, and in which the whole ethnic group performed all the tasks, economic and social, which the community required. How, when ethnic and industrial groups are coincident? When ethnic and social groups are coincident? For there is a marked tendency in the United States for the industrial and social stratification to follow ethnic lines. The first immigrants in the land simply through the accident of being first, have become its aristocracy, its chief protagonists of the pride of blood as well as of the pride of pelf, its formers and leaders of opinion, the standard-givers of its culture. Primacy in time has given them, like all "first-born," primacy in status, so that what we call the tradition and spirit of America pertains most conspicuously to them. The non-British elements of the population have been practically voiceless, but they are massive, "barbarian hordes" as the more lettered of the Americans say sometimes, and the

effect, the unconscious and spontaneous effect of
their pressure, has been the throwing back of
the Brito-American upon his ancestry and ancestral ideals. This has taken two forms: first, the
"patriotic" societies—not so much the Cincinnati,
or the Artillery Company, as those that have
arisen with the great migrations, the Sons and
the Daughters of the American Revolution, the
Colonial Dames and so on; second, the specific
clan or tribal associations consisting of families
tracing their stock back to the same pre-Revolu-
tionary ancestry—the societies of the descendants
of John Alden, etc., etc. Among these, ancient
hatred of England, so persistent in the Irish, is
completely gone. Wherever possible, the ancestral line is traced across the water to England;
old actual or heraldically designated ancestral
homes are bought; and those of the forbears of
national heroes like John Harvard or George
Washington become converted into shrines.
More and more public emphasis has been placed
upon the unity of the English and American
stock—the common interests of the "Anglo-
Saxon" nations, and "Anglo-Saxon" civilization,
the unity of the political, literary and social tradition. If all this is not ethnic nationality returned
to consciousness, what is it?

Next in general estimation come the Germans
and the Irish with the Jews a close third, although

the position of the last involves some abnormalities. Then come the Slavs and Italians and other central and south Europeans, finally the Asiatics. The Germans, as Mr. Ross points out, have largely a monopoly of brewing and baking and cabinet-making. The Irish shine in no particular industries unless it be those carried on by municipalities and public-service corporations. The Jews mass in the garment-making industries, tobacco manufacture and in the "learned professions." The Scandinavians appear to be on the same level as the Jews in the general estimation, and going up. They are farmers, mostly, and outdoor men. The Slavs are miners, metalworkers and packers. The Italians tend to fall with the negroes into the "pick and shovel brigade." Such a country-wide and urban industrial and social stratification is no more likely than the geographical and sectional stratification to facilitate the coming of "the American race!" And as American political and "reforming" action is directed upon symptoms rather than upon fundamental causes, the stratification, as the country moves toward the inevitable equilibrium between wealth and population, will tend to grow more rigid rather than less. Thus far the pressure of immigration alone has kept the strata from hardening. Eliminate that and there may be set in motion the formation of a caste system based on ethnic diversity and mitigated to only a negligible degree by economic differences.

v

The array of forces for and against that likemindedness which is the stuff and essence of nationality seems to align itself as follows. For it there work social imitation of the upper by the lower classes, the facility of communications, the national pastimes of baseball and motion-picture, the mobility of population, the cheapness of printing and the public schools. Against it there work the primary ethnic and cultural differences with which the population starts, its stratification over an enormous extent of country, and most powerfully, its industrial and economic stratification. The United States are an English-speaking country but in no intimate and utter way, as is New Zealand or Australia or even Canada. English seems to Americans what Latin used to be to the Roman provinces and to the middle ages—the language of the upper and dominant class, the vehicle and symbol of culture: for much of the population it is a sort of Esperanto or Ido, a *lingua franca* necessary less in the free than the business contacts of the daily life. The American mass is composed of elementals, peasants—Mr. Ross speaks of their menacing American life with "peasantism"—with, in a word, the proletarian foundation material of all forms of civilization. Their self-consciousness as groups is comparatively weak, although their organization and control of their individual members are often very strong. This is a factor which favors their "assimilation," for the more cultivated a group is the more it is aware of its individuality, and the less willing it is to surrender that individuality— one need think only of the Puritans themselves, leaving Holland for fear of absorption into the Dutch population; of the Creoles and the Pennsylvania Germans of this country, or of the Jews, anywhere. Peasants, on the other hand, having nothing much consciously to surrender in taking over a new culture, feel no necessary break and find the transition easy. They accomplish it, other things being equal, in a generation. It is the shock of confrontation with other ethnic groups and the natural feeling of aliency reënforced by social discrimination and economic exploitation that generate in them an intenser group-consciousness, which then militates against "Americanization" by rendering more important than ever the two factors to which the spiritual expression of the proletarian has been largely confined. These factors are language and religion. Religion is, of course, no more a "universal" than language. The history of Christianity makes evident enough how religion is modified, even inverted, by race, place and time. It becomes a principle of separation, often the sole repository of the national spirit, almost always the conservator of the national language and of the tradition that is passed on with the language to succeeding generations. Among immigrants, hence, religion and language tend to be coördinate: a single expression of the spontaneous and instinctive cultural life of the masses, and the primary inward factors making against assimilation. Writers like Mr. Ross, one notes, tend to grow shrill over the competition of the parochial school with the public school, at the same time that they belittle the fact that "on Sunday Norwegian is preached in more churches in America than in Norway."

And the anxiety of such writers might find possible justification were it not that religion in these cases always does more than it intends. For it conserves the inward aspect of nationality rather than mere religion, and tends to become the center of exfoliation of a higher type of person among the peasants in the natural terms of their traditional social inheritance or *natio.* This *natio,* reaching consciousness first in a reaction against an antagonistic America, then assumes as an effect of the competition with "Americanization" spiritual forms other than religious.

The parochial school, to hold its own with the public school, gets secularized while remaining "national." *Natio* is what underlies the vehemence of the "Americanized" and the spiritual and political unrest of the Americans. It is among the significant facts of American life today; Mr. Wilson's resentment of the "hyphenated" American was at the time both righteous and pathetic. But the hyphen attaches, in things of the spirit, also to the "pure" British-American. His cultural mastery tends to be retrospective rather than prospective. At the present time there seems to be no dominant American mind other than the industrial and theological. The spirit of the land is inarticulate, not a voice but a chorus of many voices each singing a rather different tune. How to get order into this cacophony is the question for all persons who are concerned about those things which alone justify wealth and power; for all who are concerned about justice, the arts, literature, philosophy, science. What must, what can, what *shall* this cacophony become—a unison or a harmony?

For decidedly, the older America, whose voice and whose spirit were New England, has, by virtue of business, of communications, of the immigrant, gone beyond recall. Americans of British stock still are prevailingly the artists and thinkers of the land, but they work, each for himself, without common vision or ideals. They have no *ethos* any more. The older tradition has passed from a life into a memory, and the newer one, so far as it has an Anglo-Saxon base, is holding its own beside more and more formidable competitors, the expression in appropriate form of the national inheritances of the various populations concentrated in various states of the Union, populations of whom their national self-consciousness is perhaps the chief spiritual asset, as their labor-power is their chief economic asset. Think of the Creoles in the south and the French-Canadians in the north, clinging to French for countless generations and maintaining, however weakly, spiritual and social contacts with the mother-country; of the Germans with their *Deutschtum,* their *Männerchore, Turnvereine,* and *Schützenfeste;* of the generally separate Jews; of the intensely nationalistic Irish; of the Pennsylvania Germans; of the indomitably narrow Poles and even more indomitably flexible Bohemians; of the 30,000 Belgians in Wisconsin with their "Belgian" language, a mixture of Walloon and Flemish welded by reaction to a strange social environment. Except in such cases as the town of Lead, South Dakota, the great ethnic groups of proletarians, thrown upon themselves in a new setting, generate from among themselves the other social classes which Mr. Ross and his kind so sadly miss among them: their shopkeepers, their physicians, their attorneys, their journalists and their national and political leaders, who form the links between them and the greater American society. They develop their own literature or become conscious of that of the mother-country. As they grow more prosperous and "Americanized," as they become freed from the stigma of "foreigner," they develop group self-respect: the wop changes into a proud Italian, the hunky into an intensely nationalist Slav. They learn, or they recall, the spiritual heritage of their nationality. Their cultural abjectness gives way to cultural pride and the public schools, the libraries and the clubs become beset with demands for texts in the national language and literature.

The Poles are an instance worth dwelling upon. Mr. Ross's summary of them is as striking as it is monitory. There are over three million of them in the country, a backward people, prolific, brutal, priest-ridden—a "menace" to American institutions. Yet the urge that carries them in such numbers to America is not so unlike that which carried the pilgrim fathers. Next to the Jews, whom their brethren in the Polish homeland are hounding to death, the unhappiest people in Europe, exploited by both their own upper classes and the Russian or German master, they have resisted extinction at a great cost. They have clung to their religion because it was a mark of difference between them and their conquerors; because they have been taught to love liberty, they have made their language a thing of literary importance in Europe; and their aspiration, impersonal, disinterested, as it must be in America, to free Poland, to conserve the Polish spirit, seems to be the most helpful and American thing about them—the one thing that stands actually between them and brutalization through complete economic degradation. It lifts them higher than anything that in fact America offers them. The same thing is true for the Bohemians, 17,000 of them, workingmen in Chicago, paying a proportion of their wage to maintain schools in the Bohemian tongue and free thought. The same thing is true of many other groups.

How true, may be observed from a comparison of the vernacular dailies and weeklies with the yellow American newspapers which are concocted expressly for the great American masses. The content of the former, when the local news is deducted, tends to be a mass of information, political, social, scientific; sometimes translations into the vernacular of standard English writing, sometimes original work of good, often of high literary quality. The latter, when the news is deducted, consist of the sporting page and the editorial page. Both pander rather than awaken, so

that it is no wonder that in fact the intellectual
and spiritual pabulum of the great masses consists of the vernacular papers in the national
tongue. With them go also the vernacular
drama, and the thousand and one other phenomena which compose an identifiable culture,
the outward expression of that fundamental like-
mindedness wherein men are inwardly "free and
equal." This, beginning for the dumb peasant
masses in language and religion, emerges in the
other forms of life and art and tends to make
smaller or larger ethnic groups culturally autonomous, self-sustaining, and interacting as spiritual
unit with the residuum of America.

What is the cultural outcome likely to be,
under these conditions? Surely not the melting-
pot. Rather something that becomes more and
more distinct in the changing state and city life
of the last two decades, and which is most articulate and apparent among just those peoples
whom the sociologists and Americanizers are
most accustomed to praise—the Scandinavians,
the Germans, the Irish, the Jews.

It is in the area where Scandinavians are most
concentrated that Norwegian is preached on
Sunday in more churches than in Norway. That
area is Minnesota and westward, not unlike Scan-
dinavia in climate and character. There, if the
newspapers are to be trusted, the "foreign lan-

guage" taught in an increasingly larger number of high schools in Scandinavian. The constitution of the state resembles in many respects the famous Norwegian constitution of 1813. The largest city has been chosen as the "spiritual capital," if I may say so, of the Scandinavian "house of life," which the Scandinavian Foundation in America is reported to be planning to build as a center from which there are to spread through the land Scandinavian culture and ideals.

The eastern neighbor of Minnesota is Wisconsin, a region of great concentration of Germans. Is it merely a political accident that the centralization of state authority and control has been possible there to a degree heretofore unknown in this country? That the socialist organization there used to be the most powerful in the land, able to have elected the mayor of a large city and a congressman, and kept out of office only by coalition of the other parties? That German is the overwhelmingly predominant "foreign language" in the public schools and in the university? Or that the fragrance of *Deutschtum* pervades the life of the whole state? The earliest German immigrants to America were group-conscious to a high degree. They brought with them a cultural tradition and political aspiration. They wanted to found a state. If a state may be regarded as a mode of life of the mind, it cannot be said that they have altogether failed. Their language is the predominant "foreign" one throughout the Middle West. The teaching of it used to be required by law in many places, Southern Ohio and Indianapolis, for example. Their national institutions, notably the cooking, are as widespread as they are. They are organized into a great national society, the German-American Alliance, which is dedicated to the advancement of German culture and ideals. They encourage and make possible a close and more intimate contact with the fatherland. They endow Germanic museums, they facilitate and provide for exchange professorships, erect monuments to German heroes, and disseminate translations of the German classics. And there are, of course, the very excellent German vernacular press, the German theater, the German club, the German organization of life.

Similarly the Irish, dwelling in strength in Massachusetts and New York. When they began to come to the United States they were far less well off and far more passionately self-conscious than the Germans. For numbers of them America was and has remained just a center from which to plot for the freedom of Ireland. For most it was an opportunity to escape both exploitation and starvation. The way they made was made against both race and religious prejudice: in the course of it they lost much that was attractive as well as much that was unpleasant. But Americanization brought the mass of them also spiritual self-respect, and their growing prosperity both here and in Ireland is one of the forces that underlies the more inward phases of Irish Nationalism—the Gaelic movement, the Irish theater, the Irish Art Society. I omit consideration of such organized bodies as the Ancient Order of Hibernians and the Knights of Columbus, and the bearing of the Roman Catholic church on their lives. All these movements alike indicate the conversion of the negative nationalism of the hatred of England to the positive nationalism of the loving care and development of the cultural values of the Celtic spirit. A significant phase of it was the voting of Irish history into the curriculum of the high schools of Boston. In sum, once the Irish body had been fed and erected, the Irish mind demanded and generated its own peculiar form of self-realization and satisfaction.

And finally the Jews. Their attitude toward America is different in a fundamental respect from that of other immigrant nationalities. They do not come to the United States from truly native lands, lands of their proper *natio* and culture. They come from lands of sojourn where they have been for ages treated as foreigners, at most as semi-citizens, subject to disabilities and persecutions. They come with no political aspirations against the peace of other states such as move the Irish, the Poles, the Bohemians. They come with the intention to be completely incorporated into the body-politic of the state. They alone, as Mr. H. G. Wells notes, of all the immigrant peoples have made spontaneous conscious and organized efforts to prepare themselves and their brethren for the responsibilities of American citizenship. There is hardly a considerable municipality in the land, where Jews inhabit, that has not its Hebrew Institute or its Educational Alliance, or its Young Men's Hebrew Association, or its Community House, especially dedicated to this task. They show the highest percentage of naturalization, according to Mr. Ross's tables, and he concedes that they have benefited politics. Yet of all group-conscious peoples they are the most group-conscious. Of all immigrants they have the oldest civilized tradition, they are longest accustomed to living under law, and are at the outset the most eager and the most successful in eliminating the removable differences between themselves and their social environment. Even their religion is flexible and accommodating as that of the Christian sectaries is not, for change involves no change in doctrine, only in mode of life. Yet—once the wolf is driven from the door

and the Jewish immigrant takes his place in
American society a free man (as American *mores*
establish freedom) and an American, he tends to
become rather the more a Jew. The cultural
unity of his race, history and background, is only
continued by the new life under the new conditions. Mr. H. G. Wells calls the Jewish quarter
in New York a city within a city, and more cor-
rectly than other quarters because, although it is
far more in tune with Americanism than the
other quarters, it is also far more autonomous in
spirit and self-conscious in culture. It has had its
sectaries, its radicals, its artists, its literati; its
press, its literature, its theater, its Yiddish and
its Hebrew, its Talmudical Colleges and its Hebrew Schools, its charities and its vanities, and its
coördinating organization, the Kehilla, all more
or less reduplicated wherever Jews congregate in
mass. Here not religion alone, but the whole
world of liberated thinking carries the mother
tongue and the father tongue, with all that they
imply. Unlike the parochial schools, their separate schools, being national, do not displace the
public schools. They supplement the public
schools. The Jewish ardor for pure learning is
notorious. And again, as was the case with the
Scandinavians, the Germans, the Irish, democracy applied to education has given the Jews
their will that Hebrew shall be coördinate with

French and German in the Regents' examination. On a national scale of organization there is the American Jewish Committee, the Jewish Historical Society, the Jewish Publication Society. Rurally there is the model Association of Jewish Farmers, with their coöperative organization for agriculture and for agricultural education. In sum, the most eagerly American of the immigrant groups are also the most autonomous and self-conscious in spirit and culture.

Immigrants appear to pass through four phases in the course of being automatically Americanized. In the first phase they exhibit economic eagerness, the greedy hunger of the unfed. Since external differences are a handicap in the economic struggle, they "assimilate," seeking thus to facilitate the attainment of economic independence. Once the proletarian level of such independence is reached, the process of assimilation slows down and tends to come to a stop. The immigrant group is still a national group, modified, sometimes improved, by environmental influences, but otherwise a solidary spiritual unit, which is seeking to find its way out on its own social level. This search brings to light permanent group distinctions and the immigrant, like the Anglo-Saxon American, is thrown back upon himself and his ancestry. Then a process of dissimilation begins. The arts, life and ideals of the nationality become central and paramount; ethnic and national differences change in status from disadvantages to distinctions. All the while the immigrant has been uttering his life in the English language and behaving like an American in matters economic and political, and continues to do so. The institutions of the Republic have become the liberating cause and the background for the rise of the cultural consciousness and social autonomy of the immigrant Irishman, German, Scandinavian, Jew, Pole or Bohemian. On the whole, the automatic processes of Americanization have not repressed nationality. These processes have liberated nationality, and more or less gratified it.

Hence, what troubles Mr. Ross and so many other American citizens of British stock is not really inequality; what troubles them is *difference*. Only things that are *alike* in fact and not abstractly, and only men that are alike in origin and in feeling and not abstractly, can possess the equality which maintains that inward unanimity of sentiment and outlook which make a homogeneous national culture. The writers of the American Declaration of Independence and of the Constitution of the United States were not confronted by the practical fact of ethnic dissimilarity among the whites of the country. Their descendants are confronted by it. Its existence, ac-

ceptance and development are some of the inevitable consequences of the democratic principle
on which the American theory of government is
based, and the result at the present writing is to
many worthies very unpleasant. Democratism
and the federal principle have worked together
with economic greed and ethnic snobbishness to
people the land with all the nationalities of
Europe, and to convert the early American
nationality into the present American *nation*.
For in effect the United States are in the process
of becoming a federal state not merely as a union
of geographical and administrative unities, but
also as a coöperation of cultural diversities, as a
federation or commonwealth of national cultures.

Given, in the economic order, the principle of
laissez-faire applied to a capitalistic society, in
contrast with the manorial and guild systems of
the past and the socialistic utopias of the future,
the economic consequences are the same, whether
in America, full of all Europe, or in Britain, full
of the English, Scotch and Welsh. Given, in the
political order, the principles that all men are
equal and that each, consequently, under the law
at least, shall have the opportunity to make the
most of himself, the control of the machinery of
government by the plutocracy is a foregone conclusion. *Laissez-faire* coupled with unprecedented bountiful natural resources has turned

the minds of people and government to wealth alone, and in the haste to accumulate wealth considerations of human quality have been neglected and forgotten, the action of government has been remedial rather than constructive, and Mr. Ross's "peasantism" or the growth of an expropriated, degraded industrial class, dependent on the factory rather than on land, has been rapid and vexatious.

The problems which these conditions give rise to are important, but not of primary importance. Although they have occupied the minds of all American political theorists, they are problems of means, of instruments, not of ends. They concern the conditions of life, not the *kind of life,* and there appears to have been a general assumption that only one kind of human life is possible in the United States of America. But the same democracy which underlies the evils of the economic order underlies also the evils, and the promise, of the cultural order. Because no individual is merely an individual, the political autonomy of the individual has presaged and is beginning to realize in these United States the spiritual autonomy of his group. The process is as yet far from fruition. America is, in fact, at the parting of the ways. Two genuine social alternatives are before Americans, either of which they may realize if they will. In social construction the will is father to the fact, for the fact is hardly ever anything more, under the grace of accident and luck, than the concord or conflict of wills. What do Americans *will* to make of the United States—a unison, singing the old British theme "America," the America of the New England School? or a harmony, in which that theme shall be dominant, perhaps, among others, but one among many, not the only one?

The mind reverts helplessly to the historic attempts at unison in Europe—the heroic failure of the pan-Hellenists, of the Romans, the disintegration and the diversification of the Christian church, for a time the most successful unison in history; the present-day failures of Germany and of Russia. In the United States, however, the whole social situation is favorable as it has never been at any time elsewhere—everything is favorable but the basic law of America itself, and the spirit of the American institutions. To achieve unison—it can be achieved—would be to violate these. For the end determines the means and the means transmute the end, and this end would involve no other means than those used by Germany in Poland, in Schleswig-Holstein, and Alsace-Lorraine; by Russia in the Jewish Pale, in Poland, in Finland; by Austria among the Slavs; by Turkey among the Arabs, Armenians and Greeks. Fundamentally it would require the complete nationalization of education, the abolition of every form of parochial and private school, the abolition of instruction in other tongues than English, and the concentration of the teaching of history and literature upon the English tradition. The other institutions of society would require treatment analogous to that administered by Germany to her European acquisitions. And all of this, even if meeting with no resistance, would not completely guarantee the survival as a unison of the older Americanism. For the program would be applied to diverse ethnic types under changing conditions, and the reconstruction that, with the best will, they might spontaneously make of the tradition would more likely than not be a far cry from the original. It is, already.

The notion that the program might be realized by radical and even forced miscegenation, by the creation of the melting-pot by law, and thus by the development of the new "American race" is, as Mr. Ross points out, as mystically optimistic as it is ignorant. In historic times so far as is known no new ethnic types have originated, and from what is known of breeding there comes no assurance that the old types will disappear in favor of the new. Rather will there be an addition of a new type, if it is stable and succeeds in surviving, to the already existing older ones.

Biologically, life does not unify; biologically life diversifies; and it is sheer ignorance to apply social analogies to biological processes. In any event, we know what the qualities and capacities of existing types are; we know how by education to do something toward the conversion of what is evil in them and the conservation of what is good. "The American race" is a totally unknown thing; to presume that it will be better because (if we like to persist in the illusion that it is coming) it will be later, is no different from imagining that contemporary Poland is better than ancient Greece. There is nothing more to be said to the pious stupidity that identifies recency with goodness. The unison to be achieved cannot be a unison of ethnic types. It must be, if it is to be at all, a unison of social and historic interests, established by the complete cutting-off of the ancestral memories of the American populations, the enforced, exclusive use of the English language and English and American history in the schools and in the daily life.

The attainment of the other alternative, a harmony, also requires concerted public action. But the action would do no violence to the ideals of American fundamental law and the spirit of American institutions nor to the qualities of men. It would seek simply to eliminate the waste and the stupidity of the social organization, by way of freeing and strengthening the strong forces actually in operation. Taking for its point of departure the existing ethnic and cultural groups it would seek to provide conditions under which each might attain the cultural perfection that is *proper to its kind*. The provision of such conditions has been said to be the primary intent of American fundamental law and the function of American institutions. And all of the various nationalities which compose the American nation must be taught first of all this fact, which used perhaps to be, to patriotic minds, the outstanding ideal content of "Americanism"—that democracy means self-realization through self-control, self-discipline, and that one is impossible without the other. For the application of this principle, which is realized in a harmony of societies, there are European analogies also. I omit Austria and Turkey, for the union of nationalities is there based more on inadequate force than on consent, and institutional establishment and the form of their organization are alien to the American. I think of Britain and of Switzerland. Great Britain is a nation of at least four nationalities— the English, Welsh, Scotch and Irish, and while British history is not unmarred by attempts at unison, both the home policy and the imperial policy have, since the Boer War, been realized more and more in the application of the principle of harmony: the strength of the kingdom and the empire have been posited more and more upon the voluntary and autonomous coöperation of the component nationalities. Switzerland is a nation of three nationalities, a republic as the United States is, far more democratically governed, concentrated in an area not much different in size, I guess, from Greater New York, with a population not far from it in total. Yet Switzerland has the most loyal citizens in Europe. Their language, literary and spiritual traditions are on the one side, German, on another, Italian, on a third side, French. And in terms of social organization, of economic prosperity, of public education, of the general level of culture, Switzerland is the most successful democracy in the world. It conserves and encourages individuality.

The reason lies, I think, in the fact that in Switzerland the conception of "natural rights" operates, consciously or unconsciously, as a generalization from the data of human nature that are inalterable. What is inalienable in the life of mankind is its intrinsic positive quality—its psycho-physical inheritance. Men may change their clothes, their politics, their wives, their religions, their philosophies, to a greater or lesser extent: they cannot change their grandfathers. Jews or Poles or Anglo-Saxons, in order to cease being Jews or Poles or Anglo-Saxons, would have to

cease to be, while they could cease to be citizens
or church members or carpenters or lawyers
without ceasing to be. The selfhood which is inalienable in them, and for the realization of which
they require "inalienable" liberty is ancestrally
determined, and the happiness which they pursue
has its form implied in ancestral endowment.
This is what, actually, democracy in operation
assumes. There are human capacities which it
is the function of the state to liberate and to pro-
tect in growth; and the failure of the state as a
government to accomplish this automatically
makes for its abolition. Government, the state,
under the democratic conception is, it cannot be
too often repeated, merely an instrument, not
an end. That it is often an abused instrument,
that it is often seized by the powers that prey,
that it makes frequent mistakes and considers
only secondary ends, surface needs, which vary
from moment to moment, of course is obvious:
hence the social and political messes government is always getting into. But that it is an
instrument, flexibly adjustable to changing life,
changing opinion and needs, the whole modern
electoral organization and party system declare.
And as intelligence and wisdom prevail over
"politics" and special interests, as the steady and
continuous pressure of the "inalienable" qualities
and purposes of human groups more and more

dominate the confusion of their common life, the outlines of a possible great and truly democratic commonwealth become discernible. Its form would be that of the federal republic; its substance a democracy of nationalities, coöperating voluntarily and autonomously through common institutions in the enterprise of self-realization through the perfection of men according to their kind. The common language of the commonwealth, the language of its great tradition, would be English, but each nationality would have for its emotional and involuntary life its own peculiar dialect or speech, its own individual and inevitable esthetic and intellectual forms. The political and economic life of the commonwealth is a single unit and serves as the foundation and background for the realization of the distinctive individuality of each *natio* that composes it and of the pooling of these in a harmony above them all. Thus "American civilization" may come to mean the perfection of the coöperative harmonies of "European civilization"—the waste, the squalor and the distress of Europe being eliminated—a multiplicity in a unity, an orchestration of mankind. As in an orchestra every type of instrument has its specific *timbre* and *tonality,* founded in its substance and form; as every type has its appropriate theme and melody in the whole symphony, so in society, each ethnic group may be the natural instrument, its temper and culture may be its theme and melody and the harmony and dissonances and discords of them all may make the symphony of civilization. With this difference: a musical symphony is written before it is played; in the symphony of civilization the playing is the writing, so that there is nothing so fixed and inevitable about its progressions as in music, so that within the limits set by nature and luck they may vary at will, and the range and variety of the harmonies may become wider and richer and more beautiful—or the reverse.

But the question is, do the dominant classes in America want such a society? The alternative is actually before them. Can they choose wisely? Or will vanity blind them and fear constrain, turning the promise of freedom into the fact of tyranny, and once more vindicating the ancient habit of men and aborting the hope of the world?

III

"AMERICANIZATION" AND THE
CULTURAL PROSPECT

I

THAT the image of these United States as a
"melting-pot" might be a delusion and its imputed harmony with democracy a snare was not
an idea which, prior to the Great War, seemed
even possible to Americans, whether of the
philanthropic or the academic or the business
community. The spontaneous invincible egotism
of the group was too impenetrable and the absorption in the autochthonous interests of the national enterprise—evangelism, industrial expansion, finance and the struggle of political parties
—was too complete, either for self-observation
or for comparison with others. The admitted,
and lamented, cultural inferiority to Europe was
held to be more than compensated for by the
claim of political superiority. The patriotic sentiment, the appreciation of national character,
was concentrated in the word "democracy," and
in democracy the United States was still felt to

be the nonpareil among nations, the paragon and
avatar of a state of literally free and equal citizens, or at least, if not equal in fact, equal in opportunity for every man to become the same as
his betters. The traits of these betters were envisaged as the traits of the essential American,
and personified as Uncle Sam. The current
leaders of the community were accepted as variants of him, and each in his turn—Bryan or
Roosevelt, for example—was hailed as the "typical" American. Whoever failed to acknowledge
and to conform to this type was somehow alien,
a different order of being, not admissible to the
benefits of democracy, and fit at best to be a hewer
of wood and a drawer of water to the true Americans.

The historic name for this attitude and sentiment is Know-Nothingism. Know-Nothingism
is not, of course, an American but a human trait.
What differs from ourselves we spontaneously
set upon a different level of value. If it seems
to be strong it is called wicked and is feared; if
it is regarded as weak, it is called brutish and
exploited. Sometimes, as in the attitude toward
the negro, the emotions interpenetrate and become a sentiment focalizing the worst qualities
of each. Only watchful discipline, much suffering or rare sophistication enables us to acknowledge the equality in nature and peerage in the

community of that which is different and strange, enables us to give its individuality understanding and its character respect. Otherwise, these are won from us by conflict, not yielded by good will, and most completely so among peoples, nations, states.

That the paragon and avatar of democracy should be an exception to this rule would have been morally proper but naturally impossible. The newcomers in the United States figured significantly, therefore, only as so much cheap labor-power, not as sentient men and women with temperaments, histories and hungers, settling down as neighbors in the house next door, to make a life as well as a living. As neighbors they were "undesirable," and over the barriers raised against them only a few of them could pass into the free intimacies of the neighborly life. On the whole and in the long run, they remained in their own communities, with their churches as the focus of the common life, and their "Americanization" consisted of their compenetration into the country's economic and political pattern, and of that alone. The residue of their being, where they were freest and most at home, remained continuous with their own old-worldly inheritance. As this inheritance did not enter into the overt contacts of economics and·politics, it was ignored. Such attention as was given it, was given it as only an aspect of the struggles and rivalries in those fields of the national life, and then only to suit the occasion. Defeated parties had always the traditional animadversions to make on the political corruption and economic obstreperousness due to depraved aliens.

So, as in the new world the aliens grew in mass, number and articulation, they changed in the form and in the intensity of their consciousness. When, at last, interest was directed upon their peculiar status in the cultural complex of American life, and upon the qualities and implications of their communities for excellence and evil in American society, Europe was at war, and the hateful passions of that unhappy continent were echoing and swelling across the waters. Social intelligence, never too keen in America, got beclouded by sharp partizanship and vague fears. Anxiety over the economic significance of the immigrant was reënforced by anxiety over his social significance. A turmoil of organization and fulmination ensued, with the late Colonel Roosevelt in his usual rôle of drum-major and prophet. Protecting the immigrant; restraining him; keeping him out; compelling him to conform to ourselves; doing at least something to the immigrant and especially talking all sorts of phantasies about him, became the order of the day. Only in very rare instances was any fundamental at-

tempt made to discern the forces in American
social life with which the immigrant was involved,
and to analyze out their behavior and relationships.

And even in those cases the philosophical pre-
conceptions and national eventualities of the ethnic, economic and cultural differences of the
communities composing the complex and vivid
pattern of American nationhood could not fail
of contagion from the burning issues underlying
the civil war in Europe. One publicist,[1] grown
up in the tradition that equality and similarity
were synonymous, had, in the course of his own
reflection upon the character of civilization in the
United States, come to the realization of the
democratic significance and necessity of free diversification for groups no less than for individuals. He had grown distrustful of the uniformity
and monotony imposed by the material conditions of modern life, and had reached the conclusion that diversity was not a menace to but a
promise for democracy. Another, the late Randolph Bourne, saw his country over against the
mêlée of national rivalries in Europe as a "trans-
national America." The currents of modern life,
he thought, rendered impossible tight geographical groupings of nationality. The world's population was once more adrift. Labor had been

[1] Cf. Norman Hapgood in the *Menorah Journal.*

rendered unprecedentedly mobile. Groups were
involved in temporary as well as permanent mixings, mixings in such wise that they could maintain their distinctive cultural individualities without special territorial sovereignties or political
institutions. Thus, the great North American republic, with its free institutions and continental
spaces, was a wonderful promise of the reconciliation without the destruction of the diverse races
of Europe, one nation of many peoples. John
Dewey, regarding the same situation in the light
of the problems of education, came, although his
sense of the solidity and continuity of the ethnic
groups was much weaker than Bourne's, to very
much the same conclusion. "Such terms as Irish-
American or Hebrew-American or German-
American," he wrote in 1916, "are false terms
because they seem to assume something which is
already in existence called America, to which the
other factors may be externally hitched on. The
fact is, the genuine American, the typical American, is himself a hyphenated character. This
does not mean that he is part American and that
some foreign ingredient is then added. It means
that . . . he is international and interracial in
his make-up. He is not American plus Pole or
German. But the American is himself Pole-
German - English - French - Spanish - Italian -
Greek - Irish - Scandinavian - Bohemian - Jew—

and so on. The point is to see to it that the hyphen connects instead of separates. And this means at least that our public schools shall teach each factor to respect every other, and shall take pains to enlighten all as to the great past contributions of every strain in our composite make-up. . . . I wish our teaching of American history in the schools would take more account of the great waves of migration by which our land for over three centuries has been continuously built up, and make every pupil conscious of the rich breadth of our national make-up. When every pupil recognizes all the factors which have gone into our being, he will continue to prize and reverence that coming from his own past, but he will think of it as honored in being simply one factor in forming a whole nobler and finer than itself. In short, unless our education is nationalized in a way which recognizes that the peculiarity of our nationalism is its internationalism, we shall breed enmity and division in our frantic efforts to secure unity. . . . Since as a nation we are composed of the representatives of all nations who have come here to live in peace with one another and to escape the enmities and jealousies which characterize old-world nations, to nationalize our education means to make it an instrument in the active and constant suppression of the war-spirit and in the positive cultivation of sentiments of respect and friendship for all men and women, wherever they live."

Dewey, Hapgood, Bourne, could not but be the exceptions. Public opinion as a whole responded with the customary clamor of blind fear. It echoed almost to a man Roosevelt's demand that immigrants should be required at once to forget their past and cut themselves off from their present connections, learn English and be naturalized or expelled from the country. In the interval between America's participation in the war and the making of the peace, this sentiment grew. Its animus was not then, however, directed against the total complex of European heritages upon American soil. It was directed only against the enemy, not the friendly alien. The former was the true, the divisive hyphenate, and his language, his civilization, and his cooking [1] were equally anathema. In the beginning he was almost exclusively the German-speaking immigrant from the Central Empires; toward the end the person of any speech having origin in or acknowledging sympathy with the revolutionary All Russian Soviet Republic was joined to him. Other former denizens of these Empires, and after the Revolution in Russia, Czarist émigrés, in their societies and groupings, became to the gov-

[1] On the menus of restaurants "German-fried potatoes" became "American-fried" and sauerkraut became "liberty cabbage."

ernment objects of special appreciative regard,
while the magnification of the unique ethnic and
cultural virtues of the Allies was a pæan of advertising beyond words. All these appreciations,
all these emphatic hyphenations, were of course,
to a large degree war phenomena, instruments
and engines in the warfare of propaganda and
morale abroad, devices and agencies in the business of financing and espionage at home. The
Poles, the Jews, the Czechs, the Italians, the
Greeks, every nationality represented in appreciable numbers on these shores, became the subjects of intriguing consideration to their brethren
abroad, and of solicitous interest to their government at home. Indeed, the departments of government changed toward these nationalities, as it
were, overnight, from an attitude of *laissez faire*
to an attitude of hysterical interference and
manipulation. From the Postmaster General,
from the Secretary of Labor, of State, of the
Treasury, and from the Attorney General, there
came upon them a flood of concerned and confus-
ing attention. On the one hand, their publications were coerced, controlled or suppressed; on
the other, they were invited to fill their columns
with items of public information fabricated *ad
hoc*. On the one hand, their racial and national
associations were used to effect American policies in Austria-Hungary, in Germany, in Rus-

sia; on the other their meetings were raided and
their members unlawfully arrested and jailed.
On the one hand their social organizations and
linguistic facilities were being drafted to sell
liberty bonds and thrift stamps; on the other,
their members were being defrauded and reduced
to penury by the Office of the Alien Property
Custodian. On the one hand their brethren
abroad were declared the cherished beneficiaries
of the American program of democracy and self-
determination; on the other, they themselves were
filled with "under cover" agents of Mr. Palmer's
Department of Justice and denounced for the
slightest deviation from conventional opinion by
one or more of the 250,000-odd members of its
voluntary spy-system, the "Citizens' Protective
Association."

Among the legion of unconscious comedies
which the officers of government perpetrated,
none was so comic—or so pitiful—as the confusion of public policy and the aggravation of alien
terrors they so successfully accomplished during
the war. The defense of the most trivial "rights"
of nationality abroad, the violation of the most
basic rights of man at home; collusion with nationalist organizations in foreign policy, suppression of even the religious use of their national
speech in domestic policy; a draft army one third
of whose numbers is foreign born; persecution of

the brothers, the wives, the fathers and mothers and uncles and cousins of this soldiery because they are foreign born—such is the war-time behavior of the government, preparing for a long war. Then, suddenly, the armistice: the rising and unexhausted tide of propaganda-drunk, warlike emotion unexpectedly deprived of its object; its projection upon the "reds" in place of the Germans; its elaboration by the Attorney General's Okhrana into the witch-hunting red hysteria; illegal seizures; frame-ups; persecutions; third degrees; deportations; on all sides great groups of people thrown back upon themselves, rendered fearful of their neighbors, fearful of each other, fearful of the government; on all sides driven into a state of feeling that must, undispelled, progressively insulate them against any sort of assimilation into the American community.

This feeling, which was an induction from the mass-feeling, continually whipped to new intensity by the reptile press, of the more or less native Americans, impelled immigrants to seize the first opportunity to flee the country. They preferred the security of Europe in destruction to the insecurity of the "law-and-order" lynching bees of government departments, newspapers and 100 per cent Americanist mobs. Four hundred thousand of them left for the countries of their origin in the second year of the armistice, the governments of some of these countries, like Poland, stimulating and facilitating the return of their nationals; the governments of all, even of Britain, exhibiting a hitherto non-existent concern about their movements, cultural development and social destiny.

II

The mass-feeling of the more or less native Americans found another and far more significant pattern of self-expression than that of government confusion and mob-turmoil. Like all deep and wide-ranging public emotion, it came to rest in an ideology, an orthodoxy of dogma to which all were to conform, whether freely or under compulsion. This orthodoxy was integrated and focalized in the term "Americanization." By means of it feeling was articulated in formula and restlessness drawn into a channel wherein it became policy. Between the indefinitely distensible formulæ of Americanization and the restricted channels of possible execution there was a Rabelaisian contrast. For the formulæ, being purely discharges of feeling unrestrained by fact, only served to make conspicuous the irrationality, the extravagance, and hysteria usual in such phenomena; while action, being, when it is sincere and not either politic or mad, of necessity relevant to fact, tended, wherever it really occurred, to deflate the formulæ to dimensions of sanity and to convert them from devices for the salvation of the panic-stricken into descriptions of the machinery of group adjustment for the reasonable. The formulæ were monstrous birth cries for the parturition of such a mouse of real action. Thus, the Superintendent of the Public Schools of New York City, describing in August, 1918, what must be meant by Americanization, called it "broadly speaking . . . an appreciation of the institutions of this country, absolute forgetfulness of all obligations or connections with other countries because of descent or birth." [1] This commandment expressed the tension and temper of innumerable traders, manufacturers and bankers and their derivative economic groups, such as newspaper-writers, clerks, congressmen, and other politicians, school committees and their superintendents or shop managers, and all others who were and who knew they were in a relation of organic dependence on the first group. "The institutions of this country" had a special signification for them: they were not the institutions in the totality of their diversified function and import in the national life; they were the institutions in so far and only

[1] Reported in the *New York Evening Post,* August 9, 1918.

in so far as they served to maintain the privileged
classes in America secure in their privileges.
These classes have no direct apprehension of the
psyche of any social or ethnic group other than
their own. They are proverbially timid, and they
act and talk on fear far more than on need, and
on need far oftener than on understanding.
What they knew about the immigrant was neither
seen, nor heard, nor encountered; it was transmitted in words by a specious press,[1] anxious
about its advertising, an oratorical rotary club,
a scared chamber of commerce, social club, or
defense society organized *ad hoc* Most frequently it was the broadside of a sinister economic
or political interest. It came to the Americaniz-
ing classes at three or four or fourteen removes

[1] The most illuminating record for the period in article, story
and cartoon is that of the *Saturday Evening Post*—one of the
largest and most expensive advertising sheets in America. To
these may be added the utterances of such organizations as the
industrial department of the Young Men's Christian Association
and its head, Dr. Peter Roberts; the industrial committee of
the North American Civic League for Immigrants; the latter's
subsidiary, Order and Liberty Alliance; the National Security
League; the United Americans; the Ku Klux Klan; the Loyal
American League; the National American Council, whose president is David Jayne Hill; whose vice-presidents are Charles D.
Orth of the National Security League, F. W. Galbraith of the
American Legion, Albert E. Shiels of the Inter-Racial Council,
and whose constituent organizations are the Constitutional League
of America, the Inter-Racial Council, the American Legion, the
Veterans of Foreign Wars, the Sons of the American Revolution,
the Daughters of the American Revolution, the Daughters of 1812,
the American Defense Society, the Constitutional Defense League,
the National Security League, the Chamber of Commerce of the
United States.

from the living realities of person and association among the alien groups.

It contrasts sharply in content and purpose with the formulæ of the Americanization movements which have won genuine success. Take, for example, the Americanization activities of the State of Delaware. These were a coöperative undertaking of the State and a number of interested private citizens. In a collection called *Voices of the New America* the Director of the body of volunteers calling themselves "Service Citizens" writes as follows:

"If to Americanize the immigrant means to make him into a New England Puritan, or an aristocrat of the F. F. V., or a cowboy of the far West, or any one of a score of other distinctive types, there are many good Americans who may doubt the worth of the transmutation. America is what it is, not by reason of what the earlier immigrants found here but by what they brought with them. They have never really blended, but they have developed the habit of sharing their possessions. Inter-racial tolerance is our chief virtue.

"Wherever there has been failure in what is known as the process of Americanization, the failure has come from a local breakdown of toleration. In recent years the strain placed upon

the quality has been extremely heavy. Whatever success the Delaware Americanization Committee has attained—and it is considerable—must
be attributed to the fine manner in which its officers have recognized the gifts in the hands of
the newcomers. They did not expect the aliens
to blend as by magic and become something
mysteriously and mystically different—Anglo-
Saxon, for instance; they were not expecting to
merge the variants and produce a new national
and spiritual synthesis; they were content if they
could fit the multiform and many-colored bits of
humanity into a mosaic with a fairly well-defined
pattern.

"When the wistful, confused and nervous
groups of foreigners came together for instruction, they were not instantly and contemptuously
stripped of their heritage of racial pride, traditions, customs, folk lore and music. Twenty-one
nationalities came together in evening classes, in
social gatherings, in mass meetings and every racial trait was respected. They danced the joyous
steps of the old homeland, they wore the costumes
of their native festivals, they sang the songs of
their ancestral hopes and fears. Probably every
one of them had fled from Europe or Asia to
escape some ban or tyrannous prohibition; what
love could grow in their hearts for America if

met on its threshold by a series of repressions? The highway of liberty must not be impeded by barricades.

"Perhaps it is highly important that these aliens should be naturalized, but the form of citizenship is of slight value if the citizens bring bitterness and resentment into the body politic. The Americanization policy of both the Service citizens of Delaware and the State Board of Education has been a frank recognition that even the aliens have 'certain inalienable rights.' In slightly more than a year, one hundred and thirteen pupils of the night schools have become citizens and two hundred and nineteen have taken out their first papers; they have done it without constraint—eagerly, joyously, gratefully; they have cast aside all reserve and proclaimed publicly why they love America."

A number of other states, particularly California, acted with the same good will and with a far wider range of interests affected, though not with the same expressed insight as Delaware.[1] A similar spirit was evinced, under the intelligent guidance of the late Franklin K. Lane, in the work in Americanization conducted by the Bureau of Education of the Department of the

[1] See Reports and Publications of the Commission on Immigration and Housing of California, 1919-1921. Mr. Simon J. Lubin, distinguished son of a distinguished father, was long chairman of this Commission and its guiding spirit.

Interior. Envisaging America as a system of ideals in which democracy is prepotent, it held Americanization to be a process, not of the repression, but of the protection and education of aliens—and of Americans; a process of free trade in culture, of reciprocity, mutuality and coöperation.[1] "As to our duty," Mr. Lane wrote then in his annual report to the President, "it grows out of our loyalty to ourselves, *noblesse oblige.* But we may look beyond these and find a finer reason for doing all in our power to reveal America to this man [the immigrant]. He is a human being whom we can help to a truer view of that which we have said before the world was the most stimulating, invigorating, developing of all atmospheres, that of freedom. And the test of our democracy is in our ability to absorb that man and incorporate him into the body of our life as an American. He will learn to play the game, to stand the challenge that makes us Americans; the unfostered self-sufficiency of the man who knows his way and has learned it by fighting for it will yet be his. And we will learn from him the viewpoint of those peoples who are now wrestling in all their new-found strength and weakness to realize the long-nurtured hopes. If we are to deal wisely in

[1] See Chapter I, Bulletin No. 76 (1919), Department of the Interior, and "America, Americanism, Americanization," Government Printing Office, 1919.

this larger day we must get within that man and look out with his eyes not only upon this country but upon the land from which he came, for has not America become a foster-mother to these strugglers?"

Brave words, brave vision, and a brave and daring program to incarnate them—so far as politics and the state of public sentiment would permit. Neither permitted much. Fear was abroad in the land; nothing that was done or said that could mitigate it or dispel it received any attention from the press. Delaware and California and the Department of the Interior were ignored where they were powerful, denounced where they were not. The aliency of the alien was played up, to feed fear, which grew by what it fed on. Most of the states added to the laws already existing other laws setting cultural compulsions— mostly with respect to language—upon the immigrant. Courts denied him the guarantees of free speech; legislatures refused to permit him to practice the profession of teaching: and so on. In action, therefore, the contradictory philosophies of Americanization tended to coalesce, and so far as the attitude of press and public was concerned repression overruled reciprocity. Nebraska, Iowa, Minnesota, were more representative of public sentiment than Delaware and California. The temper of the Department of

Justice dissolved to nothing the temper of the Department of the Interior. Both demanded Americanization, but the common practical eventuality which met their demands was—instruction in the English language. For the rest, Americanization was synonymous, under penalties, with submission by the immigrant communities to the economic, social, political and cultural *status quo,* their humble acknowledgment of the overlordship and ideality of the hopes and habits of the well-to-do Americans of British stock, and complaisant industry in sustaining these. The various forms of the anti-Bolshevist mania, the open-shop movement and the other class fears and preferences that were embodied in a formula and pushed as a program were all classed as Americanization.

Specifically: to a questionnaire on the subject circulated in 1920 by the National Economic League there were returned some two hundred answers from representative "liberal" men scattered all over the United States. These answers came under the eye of the writer. They were more than anything else that I know final in the demonstration of how thoroughly unreflective, how altogether emotional and verbal, unrelated to the facts in the situation public opinion was. Although very few of the respondents had had any direct personal contact with aliens or alien

groups, the great majority of them insisted on an
unreserved conformity to the *status quo*. None
of them saw America, I will not say with John
Dewey, but with Secretary Lane, as a process
of life, America "remaining ever unfinished."
Fear could be inferred from nearly all the answers, an ungrounded anxiety about the writers'
security. Nothing else could so automatically
and uniformly have led to the demand for conformity in speech, in dress, in industrial conditions. For conformity is the appearance of security; it feeds the delusion of safety, even when
the real conditions of safety do not obtain. The
aspects of conformity are various and their ap-
praisal a matter of pure feeling. Consequently,
the judgments of the respondents regarding the
technique of Americanization were as conflicting
and irreconcilable as strong feeling always makes
judgments, even of the same person. To some, no
work could be of greater value; to others, it was
a waste of effort, a sentimental substitute for
deportation and restriction. Some wanted it carried out by emotional contagion, the fervid singing of anthems and such; others proposed the dissolution of immigrant communities, the elimination of the immigrant's leaders, the stoppage of
his press, his language, his societies; naturalization rendered difficult, immigration restricted, deportation developed. The only thing about which

there was practical unanimity was that the foreigner should be required to learn English and that both public and private agencies should engage in securing the satisfaction of this requirement. This was in the spirit of the 1919 Conference of the National Education Association, which voted for "legal provision for compulsory classes in Americanization."

The pivotal consequence of this nation-wide disturbance was the appearance of a new vocation of the derivative or secondary type, the vocation of the professional "Americanizer." The personnel of this semi-clerkly, semi-missionary craft, which was manifest in force for the first time at the Conference on Americanization called in 1919 in Washington by the Department of the Interior, was at first recruited among social workers and teachers. Almost immediately, however, the craft became a vocational category on its own account. The universities, always up to the minute in service to the State, still seething with undischarged patriotic emotion left over from—for America—a too-quickly-won war, and always ready to fill any want which a clamor of taxpayers or benefactors declare to be a want of the community, flowered in schools and departments of Americanization with the same fecundity as, barely an academic season before, they had blossomed in schools of business and such.

For a time these departments were crowded. Many potential bank-clerks, school-ma'ams, clergymen and social workers were diverted from their manifest destiny. They were put in charge of "education" and "welfare-work" in shops, factories, night schools and settlements. The Christian Associations absorbed blocks of them. Even the railroads, or at least, one, the Pennsylvania system, took credit for Americanization work because it compelled its Italian road-gangs to learn English so that they might become, as President Rea wrote, "more efficient workmen." [1] A mass of Americanization publications zoomed into being, most of it, as was inevitable, trash, dealing with everything, from teaching immigrants how to write their names to comprehensive theories of orthodox life for good, obedient Americans. There was a true intellectual ferment, conceived in fear, born in the hope of gain, grown in hysteria and trained into something like sanity by the disciplining contact with fact and the slow and still unaccomplished subsidence of war-emotion.

The latter, as it slowly ebbs, leaves behind it, on different levels of the community's life, deposits of habit or formula. Fundamentally, the position of the immigrant is more precarious than ever before in the history of the United States. In their attitude toward him, the employing

[1] Samuel Rea: *Making Americans on the Railroad.*

classes are divided. All are motivated by both
self-interest and fear, but in some self-interest
overrules, in others fear. There is, for example,
or was, the Inter-Racial Council. Its finances
were supplied by numbers of great employers
who are concerned first of all about the maintenance of the supply of cheap labor. They tend,
therefore, as against the economic fears of the
American Federation of Labor and the more
complicated anxieties of the Houses of Congress,
to favor a "liberal" immigration policy almost
as fervidly as a high tariff. They are concerned,
secondly, about keeping their labor supply cheap,
therefore submissive and pliable, and they naturally want as extensive as possible a market for
their products. To attain these results, they se-
cured control of the American Association of
Foreign Language Newspapers, and their agents
know how to coerce such papers of this class as
are not in the Association. By means of this control the Inter-Racial Council carries on as an
agency of "Americanization." It secures advertising of domestic goods in its foreign-language
press. It disseminates news of the various employers' devices for industrial government, thus
making open-shop propaganda. It sends out
plate matter of advice, exhortation and encouragement in the spirit of the views and preferences
of the governors of the Council. Of course this

spirit is selfish, but this selfishness is illuminated by at least a spark of intelligence, and has the germs of a natural good in its heart.

Fear, unlike selfishness, can have no commerce with intelligence. Like love, it is blind. Although it rationalizes its behavior and justifies self-defeating action with wise cracks and sounding phrases, its conduct nullifies understanding. It moves legislatures and administrative officials more than plain citizens, for the fortune of these is made and unmade by the law of opinion and not by the laws of things. Its popular manifestation, therefore, has been the brute violence of the American Legion and the dressed-up violence of the Ku Klux Klan, both, on the whole, too intermittent and transitory, too interwoven with post-war depression to be of much significance. It is different with the state and national legislatures and the Department of Labor. These, responding to opinion, must enact laws and establish precedents that carry on when opinion has become indifferent, and only a violent and massive shift of it can disturb the inertia of established precedent. Already before the war the tendencies toward the current modes of repression and intimidation had become manifest. Since the Armistice, they have been developed into almost public policies. The instrument which renders them effectual is the formula "likely to become a public charge." Under this formula the unnaturalized immigrant lives in constant danger of deportation. He belongs just now to the "new" migration, that is, the places of his origin are central and eastern Europe. He works for the old migration. He is the miner, the mill-worker, the stockyards man, the roadmaker and the ditchdigger. His employers, afraid of his economic Americanization, attribute this inevitable change in his economic standards and associations to his ethnic and cultural difference. They call it radicalism, Bolshevism, criminal syndicalism, or whatever the current shibboleth is that gives articulation to their fear and direction to the conduct it motivates. They contrast his labor organization with the orthodox aggregation headed by Samuel Gompers, from which he is excluded, and they demand that every possible precaution shall be taken when he enters the land that he shall be safe for the democracy of which they are the palladia and beneficiaries. Thus, the scope of immigrant exclusion has within a generation been extended from health, to literacy, to opinion. Unorthodox economic opinion they regard as always an alien importation, never a home-grown product of the soil of exploitation they have themselves prepared and cultivated. When it occurs, therefore, the saving clause of the immigration law is invoked. The alien is arrested for his imputed political opinion, held without appeal or redress, tried in secret, without due process of law, by a prosecuting immigration inspector who has also been charged with the pleasure of his arrest. Now to make assurance doubly sure, the newest immigration laws passed by Congress have been so framed as to establish once more a preponderance in numbers among the immigrants of the north European stocks. In the light of the fact that of 39 or more persons deported between 1918 and 1920 for unorthodox economic and social opinions, 27 came from England, Scotland, Ireland, Denmark, Norway and Finland, the relation between fear and intelligence comes to a glare of significance.

Meanwhile, many of the non-British communities, native and naturalized as well as alien, have been in a state of panic. Their feeling of insecurity has necessarily drawn them more compactly together, consolidated their associations, closed their ranks and given their leaders an unprecedented importance in their lives. It has called the attention of the governments of the countries of their origin to the necessity of some sort of mass protection for them, to the desirability of maintaining with them a more than accidental cultural contact and interchange. The new countries particularly, whose creation has been in a large measure due to the interest of the

government of the United States, are dependent
not only culturally but economically and politically on a keen sensitiveness of their brethren
in the North American enclaves to their hopes
and needs. Such states as Poland, Czechoslova-
kia, Lithuania, Hungary, Jugo-Slavia, Ireland,
would be bound, even if they had not before them
the examples of Great Britain, Holland, Japan,
France and the Scandinavian countries, to urge
upon groups of their race and speech in the
United States the desirability and value of the
highest degree of ethno-cultural integration.
Russians and Germans, of course, far more than
the others, have been forced into such a conception by events.

III

Only in very rare instances did a disinterested
patriotic or humanitarian concern set itself the
task of neutralizing fear and greed, and of replacing them with vision regarding the nature,
trend and future of group-adjustments in the
United States. Such an instance was the Peoples
of America Society, "an organization of Americans of all origins, which in the midst of a new
wave of Know-Nothingism, is seeking through
mutual knowledge to eliminate friction and pro-
mote good relations among the peoples of the

United States." The immigrant and ethnic organizations themselves were, in their perplexity,
overeager to justify themselves, and conceded
more than was proper, necessary, or good. Labor
unions became protagonists of "Americanization," and vied with the manufacturers' associations in appropriating the term to their special
interests. Their positive achievements in "eliminating" friction and promoting good relations
among the peoples of the United States were obscured in a fog of "labor-education" theory and a
confusion of practice. That, in such a union as
the Amalgamated Clothing Workers of America,
Poles, Lithuanians, Jews, Italians, Czechs, Letts
and Slovaks, the bitterest national feudists in the
countries of their origin, could, without any surrender of their ethnic tradition and cultural integrity, but rather through the acknowledgment
and utilization of these, develop a degree of
solidarity, coöperation and moral enthusiasm unprecedented in American labor history, went unregarded. Individuals—Jews, Syrians, Dutch-
men, and such—hurried to add their testimonials
to the standard-giving supremacy of the *homo
Americanus* in works that ranged from *The Making of an American,* by Max Ravage, to *The
Americanization of Edward Bok,* by the subject
himself. The last-named book may indeed be
regarded as the climax of the wave of gratula-

tory exhibition which Mary Antin's *Promised Land* began. Now there are signs that the ebb is at hand, and that the doctrinal pattern of autobiography for the Americanized is likely to be more analytical, discriminative, and sad.[1]

Indeed, analysis and discrimination have come more significantly to light in other forms. It is, of course, inevitable that the academic pursuit of material for a discipline looking toward a job in the gentle art of Americanization should, in some places, at some time, lead the more scholarly-minded and scientific among the professors of Americanization to forget the end in the means, and to replace racial anxiety, political expediency and moral fatuousness with a free curiosity about the patterns of group behavior under the conditions of life on the richest part of the North American continent. So far, however, the inevitable and the actual do not coincide. Ross is still the standard instance of the academic special pleader in this field, and the brilliant work of W. I. Thomas[2] and his associates still stands alone among academic productions. It is outside of the academies, among representatives of ethnic stocks disturbed about their status and

---

[1] See *Up Stream*, by Ludwig Lewisohn. More recently there has appeared a pseudo-autobiography entitled *Haunch, Paunch and Jowl*, which gives vivid point to the character of the change. The book illuminates day-to-day realities of the Americanization process.

[2] Cf. *The Polish Peasant in Europe and America.*

anxious to envisage it in a coherent philosophy
of the national life, that something approaching
to free inquiry has been undertaken, partly in the
attempt to find an intellectual way through the
emotional turmoil about Americanization. One
sought to discover how stable was the ethnic
ground of cultural diversity; [1] another, to evaluate theories of Americanization through an analysis of their bearing on the lives of the smaller communities of which the life of the country is composed.[2] Still another, surveying the whole field,
was initiated by the trustees of the Carnegie Corporation of New York and was designed "to set
forth, not theories of social betterment, but a description of the methods of the various agencies
engaged in such work." Its assumption—ironic,
in view of its conclusion—was, however, that
"Americanization is the uniting of new with native-born Americans in fuller common understanding and appreciation to secure by means of
individual and collective self-direction the highest welfare of all. Such Americanization should
perpetuate no unchangeable political, domestic
and economic régime delivered once for all to
the fathers, but a growing and broadening national life, inclusive of the best wherever found.
With all rich heritages, Americanism will de-

[1] Cf. J. Drachsler: *Democracy and Assimilation.*
[2] Cf. I. Berkson: *Theories of Americanization.*

velop best through a mutual giving and taking of contributions from both newer and older Americans in the interest of the commonweal." [1]

The upshot of the first endeavor is a compromise between Democracy and the Melting Pot, a giving unto Cæsar what is Cæsar's so that God may keep his own. The philosophy of Messrs. Drachsler and Berkson is identical. They believe that the American peoples, left to themselves, are likely to assimilate into a single stock. They believe that this blind, spontaneous assimilation is fraught with much pain and hardship, and that intelligent statesmanship would so direct it as to ease it. They also believe in democracy, and in the application of the terms of democracy to groups as well as to individuals. But they cannot stick having these groups called nationalities. They prefer to call them communities. They are plainly disturbed about the irrelevant political suggestion of the word "nationality" and are much exercised over the idea of race as an element in nationality. They show emotion about both things and are at pains to prove over again the well-known anthropological commonplaces that race is a concept the underlying facts of which are mutually contradictory, that races are indefinite and impermanent and that communities them-

[1] Parks and Miller: *Old World Traits Transplanted:* Publisher's Note.

selves dissolve. Messrs. Drachsler and Berkson
believe that even if you can't change your own
grandfather, you can modify your great-grand-
child's, by choosing for him a great-grandmother
of another stock than your own. That people are
hardly ever known to marry out of consideration
for their great-grandchildren does not seem to
have occurred to them. So Mr. Drachsler elo-
quently shows that in New York City, and by
implication in the rest of the country, a great deal
of such prospective grandpaternal modification
does take place, at least from the first to the third
immigrant generation. He has figured out that
the largest number of intermarrying persons
come from what he calls the "mediocre culture
groups," by which he means, apparently, economic groupings bringing into the greatest degree of propinquity the largest number of persons
of different ethnic stocks. "Amalgamation," Mr.
Drachsler concludes, "of the European peoples in
the United States is going on and gathering momentum on the way." Its tendency is to dilute
the native stocks, as the direction of intermarriage is from the lower to the higher social classes,
and the range of intermarriage narrows from
twelve nationalities in the first generation to six
in the second. The writer believes that the hardship which this "amalgamation" involves will be
eased if the immigrant groups conserve for

America "through voluntary cultural community
organizations, the unique value of their heritage;
while the state will find its proper function in
the harmonization of these values through a
synthetic cultural curriculum in its public educational system." The "voluntary cultural organizations" are to be called, not nationalities but
"communities" and Mr. Berkson adds to the contentions of Mr. Drachsler some further observations about communities. He believes in the
status quo and wants to leave well enough alone.
He thinks the formula of the "community" is
flexible and free. . . . "It leaves all the forces
working . . . where its alternatives presume too
much to 'fix' conditions." He wants "all forces to
be given a just opportunity to exert their influence." Thereupon, "if the ethnic group perpetu-
ates itself, reason accepts it," and "if the ethnic
group finally disintegrates, the 'community'
theory resolves itself into the 'Melting Pot'
theory, accomplishing fusion without the evils of
hasty assimilation." His panacea, in a word, is a
sort of ethnic and cultural *laissez faire.*

Of a similar, more decisional character, is the
conclusion of the Carnegie Americanization
study. Its attitude toward the purely ethnic
considerations of its problem is, however, one of
pronounced skepticism. Though "the characteristics of the Swede, the Jew, the Italian, may be

connected with their original inborn temperamental dispositions," they can never be discovered
in their originality and purity. Circumstances
modify them continually and the "primary group
organization," that which persists as an element
of all present society, and the home forms of
which immigrants spontaneously reproduce and
live in, is itself too much an interpenetration of
heredity and environment to permit of successful analysis. The point of importance is that the
immigrant penetrates the American scene from
the springboard of these basic familial associations. His adjustments to the scene are facilitated by the institutions of his group, these being,
first of all, his ethnic boarding-house, then the
banks and employment agencies, then the mutual
aid and benefit societies, finally the nationalistic
societies, like the Sons of Italy with their 125,000
members distributed in 887 lodges through 24
States, or the Polish National Alliance with its
130,000 members and 1,700 lodges, or the Japa-
nese Association of America, or the various
French Canadian and Jewish societies. The existence of all these appears to be postulated upon
the realization that "the individual will not be
respected unless his group is respected." Many
derive from a political idealism for the home-
country and therefore resent and seek to avert
Americanization—as for example, the Poles,

some of whose leaders call them "a Polonia Americana, the fourth division of Poland"—and draw their intellectual sustenance entirely from the home country.

But regardless of whether their spirit is that of the colonist merely or of the settler come "to secure an existence," they automatically Americanize, and their own organizations are the chief instruments in the process. For without them the immigrant would be completely lost. They both ease his transition and speed it. Although he can swiftly change his clothes and his superficial manners, thus throwing off the external differences between himself and his new *milieu,* the inner change, the conversion of habit and attitude are another story, and it is in this story that the immigrant's institutions are the hero. In the new community his old habits and attitudes do not obtain the old results, and the old results are no longer successful adjustments in the situation. The immigrant's personality suffers attrition and dislocation. He doesn't belong, and so, cannot find himself. Disjoined from the old ways and values and not yet at home in the new, he becomes demoralized. Just in so far as he can live and move and have his being in the groupings of his own people he is saved, however, from the consequences of his demoralization. The groupings are his organs of contact with the new social *milieu.*

They speak his language and convey his ideas; they speak the language of the land and communicate its moods. They are the intermediaries between him and it. They carry him over and ultimately they adjust him.

In this mediating relationship, language is perhaps the most important of all the elements. It is the intimate symbol of association; so far as the immigrant is concerned, its warmest and most significant base. Race, in fact, is often hardly more than a linguistic term. For this reason the immigrant or foreign-language press becomes one of the nodal immigrant institutions. Forty-three or forty-four dialects are spoken in the United States and more foreign journals are published and read in more languages per capita than in the whole of Europe. They serve their readers with news of the countries of their origin, and help adjust them to the country of their habitation; and they are used—in all cases except that of the Jews—for the purpose of preserving or aggrandizing one or another nationality abroad. They have a political import for foreign policy which the world war should have mitigated. Their cultural significance is low. As their readers are mostly peasants, they tend to stay upon the level of the American yellows. They print some poetry, much sentimental fiction, and they often come under the domination of advertisers—to

say nothing of the politicians. There are exceptions, of course. The Yiddish press tends on the
whole to maintain a superior intellectual level,
and the "radical" press of all nationalities is filled
with disquisitions beyond the mind of the average
reader. But the literary quality of the foreign-
language press has no particular influence upon
its social function—the newcomer's graduation
into American life. This it serves efficiently.
The graduation takes place.

Mr. Gavit's study of naturalization shows [1]
that the immigrant of the new migration is as
eager, and more eager, to enter into the fullness of
American citizenship as the immigrant of the old.
The inferences and conclusions which his comprehensive survey of all the available data has enabled him to draw are to the effect that the presumption that the later migration is of a worse
character than the earlier is a pure myth; so is the
notion current that the later migration is less
amenable to citizenship; or that it differs from the
older migration in anything but "the political, social and economic conditions at the time of migration in the country of origin." All that can be
discovered as "the controlling factor in political
absorption is length of residence." The process
of naturalization is a phenomenon altogether independent of racial origin and altogether de-

[1] "Americans by Choice," *The Survey*, February 25, 1922.

pendent on economic status: "the racial groups
show a slower desire for citizenship and a slower
rate of naturalization while they are employed
in the more poorly paid industries; both the individual interest and the rate increase as the individuals toil upward in the social and economic
scale. . . . Those from countries where at the
time of their migration there was either auto-
cratic government or political discontent or inferior economic opportunity, head the list of those
who seek, and upon examination prove, their title
to fellow-membership with us."

"Assimilation," Mr. Parks concludes,[1] and his
conclusion is a fit summary for the study, "is as
inevitable as it is desirable; it is impossible for
the immigrants we receive to remain permanently
in separate groups. Through point after point
of contact, as they find situations in America intelligible to them in the light of the old knowledge and experience, they identify themselves
with us. We can delay or hasten this development. We cannot stop it. If we give the immigrants a favorable *milieu,* if we tolerate their
strangeness during their period of adjustment,
if we give them freedom to make their own connections between old and new experiences, if we
help them to find points of contact, then we hasten
their assimilation. This is a process of growth,

[1] *Old World Traits Transplanted.*

as against the 'ordering and forbidding' policy
and the demand that the assimilation of the immigrant shall be "sudden, complete and bitter."
And this is the completely democratic process,
for we cannot have a political democracy unless
we have a social democracy also."

IV

That time—he, the notorious healer of all hurt
—will put a period to the public sentiment underlying the Americanization hysteria and shift the
approval of public opinion from the coercive to
the persuasive conception of public policy regarding the integration of immigrant groups and native society, is by no means a foregone conclusion.
The causes of disturbance are as varied as they
are lasting. Their repression on one side leads
most of the time only to their protrusion on another. Alone the coincidence of ethnic differences with economic stratification is enough to
exacerbate a condition which, with the pressure
of immigration removed, must of necessity tend
toward fixation. One need only cast an eye over
the negro-white relations in the South to realize
the limit that such a condition would, unchecked,
engender. And even checked, with all the heal-
ing that time might bring, the current of public
sentiment would still have left institutional de-

posits, have set up interests and organizations whose pattern of behavior and endeavor to survive would be postulated upon this sentiment. The Americanizers and the Americanization agencies are themselves such interests and organizations. Such, also, the immigrant institutions, now reënforced and sustained by the solicitude of the new and old governments abroad, have been compelled to become. These, and the protective reactions which they express against the assault of the public sentiment to which they are in part a reply, form the mutually sustaining halves of a circle; a complete, a closed circle. Only a stronger sentiment of another nature can break this circle, break it either by displacing the original mood as the power sustaining the interests and organizations, or by diverting the nourishing energy of opinion into the generation and sanction of other vocations and institutions. The likelihood of such an eventuality, however, seems at present too remote. Unless it happens soon, it will happen too late.

For the Americanization emotion of 1919 was no eccentric or isolated phenomenon, no idiosyncratic aspect of war-psychology. The moods of war were added unto it, but did not create it; they intensified it, but its original force did not come from them. Nor was its source—as some, following the current fashion of interpreters of social behavior, opine—in the conflict of economic interests. Organized labor's attitude toward immigration might be so envisaged, and the passing complication of the immigrant with economic radicalism might be so envisaged. But the classes in whom the Americanization psychosis was most compulsive and outstanding were the classes whose economic interests are most fully served by un-Americanized, that is, by cheap, ignorant and slavish immigrant labor, such as Judge Gary's liberalism toward the immigrant specifically calls for. The more intelligent among these classes, such as the Inter-Racial Council, recognized this, and set themselves hard at the task of persuading their peers of it—with doubtful success. The mood of 1919 has an authenticated ancestry in the story of the persistent temper of public sentiment in the United States. It is the old Know-Nothingism in contemporary dress. This Know-Nothingism was not postulated on either economic rivalry or war anxiety. It was postulated on something more protean and more enduring, on something taboo to law and intelligence, something that even derision strengthens and scorn confirms. The something is religious tradition, the prejudice of cultus. Its language is various, but its mood is the same. It is transmitted through one of the most basic and intimate of community groupings and it goes on, from the

Massachusetts colonials to their offspring in the fourth, and even the forty and fourth, generation. It has, of course, its peaks and its valleys, its cycles of mania and depression. The post-armistice manifestations were a period of mania. The witch-hunting of the Quaker attorney-general, Palmer, the czaristically inspired Jew-baiting of the Baptist automobile maker, Ford, the malevolent mass-mummery of the Ku Klux Klan, the racial rumblings [1] of Mr. Madison Grant, Mrs. Gertrude Atherton, the *Saturday Evening Post,* are all, ultimately, manifestations of this Know-Nothingism. The economic process has, on the whole, tended to reënforce rather than to subdue it. There is the possibility that it might, by shifting the balance of social power, drain it, and finally dry it up. But this is only a possibility, and at best, a possibility of the far future. The testimony of history favors rather the cumulative integration and enhanced rate of explosion of the emotions underlying this Know-Nothingism.

Intellectuals dealing with the process and qualities of group-adjustment in the United States have altogether overlooked the psychological substructure of American Know-Nothingism, its patterns and periods. As it is the non-British,

---

[1] Directly derivative from the race-mythology imagined in Germany and elaborated for pan-Germans by Houston Stewart Chamberlain, a renegade Englishman.

not the native community, that is being thereby challenged as a menace, the attention of the intellectuals has been devoted to the analysis and dissipation of this imputed menace, and to the restoration of that complacency of conduct which is the crown of unruffled feelings. They have been content to pass by the prior question regarding the specific nature and social significance of that which the non-British communities are said to be a menace to, and which would have to absorb them and digest them, converting them into flesh of its flesh and soul of its soul, if it is to be forever inviolate and safe. Assimilation, declares the Carnegie Study, is as inevitable as it is desirable. But of what, to what? How is assimilation to be understood? As a coöperative harmony, which is the outcome of mutual respect, understanding and adjustment, on the rule of one for all and all for one, or as the dissolution and absorption of diversities, on the rule of all for one and all in one? The very language of the Study,[1] written about "foreigners" from the standpoint of the American native insecure in their presence, shows how impossible it is for the best will in the world to avoid sharing the native emotion and the native assumption that alien heritages, which are "methods of valuation," are inferior to the native and must give way to the

[1] See supra, p. 121.

native. This assumption of superiority is, of course, automatic, universal, and endemic. It is to be found everywhere that individual or group diversities confront one another. It is everywhere a defense against and an evasion of the intolerable alternative which challenges every student of civilization—the alternative, namely, that the heritage which is his, is at least not better than and perhaps not as good as the heritage which confronts his. Yet intelligence cannot be honest or effective in this field, cannot *be* intelligence, until it has learned not only to tolerate but to feel at home with this intolerable thing. Until it does, it will at bottom, like the Carnegie Study, knowingly or unknowingly, condone conformity and approve submission.

And conformity and submission are what will seem to come. But only seem. For the adaptability of life is wonderful, and communities, like persons, suffer much and surrender more, only to save their souls alive. The compulsion of native *mores* is a stimulus to which the American of non-British stock makes appropriate response. But the response is far from determined by this stimulus alone. In one way or another, that inward half of his being, the "methods of valuation," the group patternings, the consuetudinous rhythms and symbols of custom and speech that are his heritage, the springs of his character, will color and direct his response. This inward half necessarily and automatically behaves in such a way as to maintain itself and grow, and if it is prevented from doing so directly, openly, in free interplay with its social *milieu*—then, necessarily and automatically, it will do so obliquely, hiddenly, in conflict with its *milieu*. The *milieu* may exterminate it, but the *milieu* will not assimilate it. It will fight like the Irish, or recede behind the church like the Poles, or intrench itself in cult like the Pennsylvania Dutch or generate protective adaptations like the Jews. But it will not of its own will give up the ghost. It will automatically defend itself from day to day, and to gain strength concede its own failure, justify itself by the ideology of its opponents, and carry on; all with the deepest, naïvest sincerity, the greatest piety, to the ineffables of the ruling society, the utmost deference toward this society's taboos.[1] All the valuations of the majority, its idols from cave, market place, forum, closet and altar, are automatically and unconsciously used as agencies to conserve the integrity of the minority's values; formulæ are confused with facts, events with appreciations, to the end that the assault upon the

---

[1] Cf. Mr. Ludwig Lewisohn's "wealthy Jewish physician who had turned Methodist in his boyhood, avoided all questionable subjects, prayed at love feasts in the church, and, though he surreptitiously distributed alms among the poor Jews of the city, achieved a complete conformity of demeanor." He has his comrades in every race.

group's individuality may be relaxed and the group suffered to live for the present, even if eventually it must die a natural death. The sophism lies in the fact that every moment which is, is the present moment. The group changes, but it does not lose continuity, even if it loses memory; and where the continuity of life persists, the forgetting of past life may be overcome.

The treatment of such conceptions as *race, democracy,* and *culture* by the recent studies of group contacts in America mentioned earlier,[1] is a sophism of this class. It is the argument of a foregone conclusion in the light of an immediate interest rather than an ultimate eventuality, a practical deduction from a mystic and ineffable premise, wherein the inalterable concept is invoked to justify the struggling and contrary fact. As if culture, race and democracy could have any meaning apart from the shifting constellations of men and events which they designate, or could serve as programs—programs are usually given an ineffable dimension by being called ideals— apart from the ungratified or obstructed wishes they are plans to gratify and to set free!

v

First, as to the idea and uses of "race."
The late James Bryce, writing in 1892 of the

[1] Cf. supra, p. 113.

influence of immigration upon the character and institutions of the people of the United States, was inclined to make gentle fun of hereditarians. He doubted whether diverse bloods could have the importance imputed to them. He noted that the children of immigrants appeared to grow up into persons "far more like native Americans than the prevalent views of heredity would have led us to expect." He saw "in the intellectual and moral atmosphere of the United States more power to assimilate men than their race qualities have power to change it." Thirty years later, discussing the topic anew, he said:

"When two or more races mix their blood, what is the comparative importance of blood, i. e., of Heredity, on the one hand, and of Environment on the other, in determining the quality of the race which arises from the mixture? In the United States the child of Italian or Czech parents grows up ignorant but intelligent, untrained to anything but hand labor, yet inheriting certain inborn tendencies and propensities, and possibly also drawing from his parents certain beliefs and habits. The boy goes to an American school, where he imbibes the ideas and imitates the ways of the American youth around him, and as he grows up reads the same newspapers, hears the same talk. Unless his parents are well-educated persons, he is eager to forget their race and to become immediately and for all purposes an American and nothing but an American. He waves the same Stars and Stripes, he sings in the class

"My country, 'tis of thee,
Sweet land of liberty. . . ."

with more effusion than if his ancestors had come over in the 'Mayflower.' Yet the blood remains. He is not, he cannot make himself, altogether an American, divesting himself of the parental tendencies, of the emotional excitability of the Czech or the impulsiveness of the Italian. To what extent then will these racial qualities pass into and modify the American mass? How far will a crowd, twenty per cent of which is of Polish or Greek or Jewish parentage, differ from a native American crowd? When three generations have passed, how far will the population of any city, one-half of the blood in whose veins comes from East European sources, feel, think, and act differently from the way in which people in that city felt, thought and acted years ago, say in 1880, before the East European flood had swollen? The city was then four-fifths English, the rest North European or Irish. In 1960 not more than half will be of English blood, but all will be English-speaking, and permeated by American influences. Though no one can answer the question I am putting, this much, at least, may be said. There has never been anywhere an environment of more pervasive and compulsive power than that into which the immigrant is plunged when he lands in America. He seems to melt in it as a lump of sugar melts in a cup of tea. Yet one cannot but believe that the influence of heredity remains. If we discern racial traits in the individual man and explain points in his character by saying he has a strain of Greek or Polish or Jewish blood, must not the inherited quality of the individuals modify the quality of the mass?

"The question can never be fully answered, because causes other than heredity are always modifying national character from one age to another. When, sixty years hence, observers compare the character of the American of 1980 with that of the American of 1880, it will be impossible to determine how much of the change is due to this particular cause. The character of a nation, like that of an individual, is always undergoing changes too subtle to be discernible at any given moment, but evident after a lapse of years. They are retarded or accelerated in the political sphere by the presence or absence of the institutions and traditions which are continually forming men's habits of thought and action, making the habits flow in certain channels and deepening those channels. But it must be remembered that institutions themselves are always changing, if not in their form yet in the manner of their working. Nothing can arrest either growth or decay except death, and health consists in the power of eliminating the dying tissues and replacing them by those in which life is vigorous.

"Thoughtful men in America are disquieted when they see under their eyes a change passing upon the elements in the population far greater than has ever passed before upon the English stock since it came to Britain in the fifth century of our era. Some fear a permanent injury to the moral, perhaps even the intellectual quality of the stock. Others believe that the power of literature and education and the old traditions of the nation will preserve what is best in the essentials of character. Uncertain as the future is, one who has watched the process during many years finds reason for sharing the more hopeful belief."

From the negation or neutralization of heredity to the acknowledgment of its persistence and influence is no inconsiderable step. Yet Mr. Bryce has taken it and it is a wise step. It is a step supported by such anthropological evidence as exists to-day. Intermarriage or no intermarriage, racial quality persists, and is identifiable, as Mr. Bryce recognizes, to the end of the generations. For the purposes of any but Laputan statesmanship, different races responding to the same stimuli are still different, and no environmental influence subtle as thought and overwhelming as a tank can ever remold them into an indifferent sameness. It may scatter them. It may neutralize and so nullify their traits. It may overlay and repress their traits. But it cannot identify their traits. Identity may be a limit which, like the heads of New York Jews and Sicilians that Mr. Boas measured, races approach, but which they never attain. Intermarriage, consequently, is not racial assimilation. Three hundred years of fusion of the white peoples inhabiting the North American continent has not produced a blend which may be called a new race,[1] and there exists no valid reason for supposing that it is likely to. The older types persist, and there is nothing to keep them from so continuing on any principle of the relation of heredity to environment that may be applied to them. New types come as additions to the old, and only extreme alterations of *milieu,* cataclysmal mutations incompatible with their survival, can destroy them. So far, the differences between the North American and the European continents have not amounted to such changes. Winters are colder

[1] Cf. Alex. Hrdlicka in the *Journal of Heredity*, VI., Nov. 1914, and "Study of Old Americans" in the *Proceedings of the XIXth Int. Congress of Anthropology,* 1917.

in America and summers warmer. There are continental topographical differences between the Atlantic coast-line, the Appalachian range, the great midland plains, the western plateaus, the Rockies and the Pacific Coast. Latitude 35 degrees N. is a climatic dividing line between North and South. These diversities of topography and climate lead of themselves to observable and explicit diversifications of economy, of speech, of tradition, of outlook. And these diversifications are only institutional, not racial. In fact, the natural setting, unmodified, would enhance the institutional variation; it would of itself reject uniformity. At those points where experience is most intimate, cumulative and compelling, in the immediacies of daily life, it does make for variation. But the natural settings of the continent, with their diversity, are confronted with the artificial settings of the works of man. These fabricated obstructions to variation have never been so massive or so forceful. Their fundament is machinery. Railroads and tractors, telephones and movies, phonographs and radios, school systems and political establishments, lay upon the continental ranges of the American state a uniformity without precedent and without parallel.

What is important, however, is the fact that the uniformity is superimposed, not inwardly generated. Under its regimentation the diversi-

ties persist; upon it and by means of it they grow.
But instead of growing freely, and fusing by
their own expansion into contact and harmony
with their peers, they grow distortedly, as reactions against and compensations for the superimposed unity. In the end they must win free,
for Nature is naturally pluralistic; her unities are
eventual, not primary; mutual adjustments, not
regimentations of superior force. Human institutions have the same character. Where there is
no mutuality there may be "law and order" but
there cannot be peace.

Broadly speaking, what is true of institutions
is also true of race. Speculation has it that the
races of man are diversified fruits of a single
seed. They have crossed, separated and recrossed
from before history, and they have grown in number and in kind. They have been wanderers and
they have been settlers. Each has been the
maker, the bearer, the robber, the imitator, the
destroyer of various cultures. Each has sustained something, rejected much, assimilated
something from the works of man about him.
Each has given to what it has successfully assimilated, by the very fact of success, that twist of
difference from its past, that mutation of nature
which rendered the thing acquired truly an utterance of its own spirit continuous with its own
past. The inspiration of the Greeks was not

Greek but Minoan, Egyptian, Persian. The
Jews borrowed from Babylon and Athens, the
Romans from Greece and all the world, the
Arabs from Byzantium and Africa. As for
modern peoples—is anything so significant of
European history as the free movement and
interchange of the cultural achievements of the
different nationalities? The intellectual and
imaginative content of the great tradition of
Europe is a common, interpenetrative store of
diverse national cultures, wherein the unique individuality of each is nourished by the unique individualities of the others. How have they grown
by what they fed on, and what have they fed on
but one another! Race, in its setting, is at best
what individualizes the common heritage, imparting to it presence, personality and force. It is to
that what an instrument is to the music of a symphony. The latter is an inert abstraction, black
marks on paper, the mere possibility of sound.
It can come to actuality and loveliness only by
virtue of the instrument that incarnates it. Its
living quality is in the timbre of the instrument,
in the skill of the player, and in these its individual uniqueness resides. An orchestra is the free
and well-ordered coöperation of unique individualities toward the making of the common tune.
There is a true division of labor in the making of
this tune, for although instruments are broadly

interchangeable, there are limits set by the timbre
to the adequacy and beauty of their utterance.
A jig on a bassoon is a joke and a funeral march
on a fife is a flivver. Timbre reacts selectively to
tunes.

In the vague way not well analyzed, and much
misrepresented, race reacts selectively to culture.
Not all cultural values circulate with the same
ease and freedom among all peoples. Economic
values appear to be the only ones that do so, particularly the values of industrial civilization.
Economic institutions pure and simple, those relatively unconditioned by climate and natural resources, tend to spread to all the places of human
habitation. Machinery and transport come to be
as indifferently in Japan as in England, in China
as in the United States, in India as in France.
By the necessities of the situation they tend to
evoke the same social groupings and to determine
human association in the same ways. It is with
respect to the free, the "useless" expressions of
group-life that varying sensibilities and imper-
meabilities become manifest, and these it is that
are creatively significant. Somehow, with all
their love of music and supremacy in poetry, the
British have never been a music-making people,
or produced a great musician of the very first
order. Somehow, the Germans have never attained supreme creative distinction in architec-

ture nor the French in poetry. Somehow, German and Italian music are not substitutes but supplements for one another. Now the music, architecture, poetry, of each of these peoples are the common heritage of all, but they cannot help accepting them differently. No trade has been freer than the free trade in cultural achievement, and in no other field has the obscure selective action of temperament appeared more definitively.

The temperamental differences, indeed, manifest themselves within the nation itself, and the cultural contrast between the northern and the southern French, or the Venetians and the Florentines, or the Dutch and the Walloons are among the pivotal unstudied data in the story of national civilizations. Has anybody yet thought to evaluate for culture in the United States the temperamental differences between Louisiana and Kansas, between Philadelphia and New York, between Wisconsin and Michigan? Different temperaments, expressed in different patterns of community life, making free adjustments to one another within the limits of a common social purpose growing out of the adjustments, appear to develop a coöperative unity which is lasting, tensile, and creative in the degree that the liberty is complete and the adjustment benevolent. Great Britain is the stock example of a country which has been constituted by diversities rather than uniformities. Idiosyncrasy has been a commonplace there, regimentation an exception, and the state of the nation has set the terms of its ideal. France, on the contrary, and, after the Franco-Prussian War, Germany, have been countries of regimentation with life focalized at the capital and so impoverished and degraded in the provinces. Britain, consequently, has shown a vitality which in its elastic cohesion, its viability, more than compensated for its lack of form. The pointed excellency of French form makes one forget French rigidity and brittleness—qualities which have ever been held as signs of decadence. Political and economic institutions which are adjusted to group idiosyncrasy appear, other things being equal, to possess traits of durability and continuity lacking in others. The spring and origin of these traits are to be looked for, of course, not on the higher levels of government or business but on the lower ones, where people live, and where their daily life is genuinely and momentously enchanneled. Thus, in the familial relations of the village community, all the world over, there prevails a significant democracy which is the dimmed original and the minatory criterion of all larger forms and subsequent variations. Deviations from that type or incompatibilities with it—as in slavery and serf-

dom and their accompanying degradations—have
led invariably to disaster to the larger forms.
There is more than sufficient ground in history,
therefore, for Mr. Bryce's optimism regarding
the power of a democratic America to absorb un-
politicated European stocks. If the United
States remains a democracy, the addition of new
temperaments to the national life, provided these
be given free play within the institutional whole,
can serve only to strengthen and to enrich it.

It is the meaning and implication of this free
play that is the problematic thing. Conceivably,
a newborn Chinese child, brought up from its
first cry in a loving Yankee family, might for all
practical purposes be a Yankee. The patterns of
its behavior and the contents of its mind would
certainly be Yankee. And if enough such in-
fants could be so brought up, they might compose a race of Mongolian Yankees. The thing
would seem far easier, less unnatural, with children of the non-Yankee European stocks. If
America be a melting-pot, this is the thing that is
done.

Only, the United States is no more, and no
less, a melting-pot than any other country in the
world. In the nature of things, none can be, for
the particular condition—just exemplified—
which might make it one is precisely the condition which can never obtain. Birth, which we do

not choose, carries with it simultaneously certain
cultural acquirements of a nature so basic, so
primary, as to be indistinguishable from inheritance. The acquirements are, in fact, the infant's
immediate social inheritance. They are the abo-
riginal impressions from the familial *milieu.*
This, with its predominantly ethnic elements,
tone and rhythms, is more than any other continuous with the past. The present substance of
the past may be rich, elaborated and various, or
thin and threadbare, but certain indefinable essentials endure. They set the infant's mind and
predetermine the direction of its later reactions
in many more and socially more significant ways
than the purely sexual with which Freud and his
school concern themselves. Particularly, they
establish the lines of association, the preferences
of the herd type in which the individual feels freest and most at ease, in which he can feel relaxed
and be at play. These appear to be prevailingly
ethnic. Italians and Jews and Yankees and
Irishmen may have become people of a single culture, tradition, aspiration and public behavior,
yet they will regularly associate with people of
their own racial and familial tone, and their marriages will not so very largely overflow the boun-
daries set by these factors and by their churches.
The United States is conspicuously marked by
groupings of this kind; among the Americans of

British stock the tendency increases to give them formal significance and an explicit familial base, and to consecrate them in the academic and social discriminations of the college life.[1] But they are to be found in all countries. In the nature of things, how could they not be found?

If any valid inference can be drawn regarding

[1] This tendency is admirably illustrated by the recent agitation among some officials and undergraduates of Harvard College over the number of Jews there. The life of that academy, like the life of all the other endowed institutions of learning in the United States, goes on in two dimensions. One is ostensibly intellectual. Its line is the instruction of the youth who are supposed to resort to colleges for the purpose of learning the art of seeking and recognizing truth. The other is social. Its line is the maintenance and elaboration of certain traditions of association, of attitude, of behavior, conditioned on the continuity of certain familial customs and relationships. The first is organized about the class-room. The second is organized about the undergraduate club or fraternity. The connection between the two forms of organization is purely external. They involve one another only through accident. The class-room form is in the main a disagreeable price which those seeking the social cachet of being "college men" must pay for the privilege of participating in the club-room form. Undergraduate feelings, interests and ambitions are integrated by the latter. The latter sets the standards and establishes the patterns of undergraduate life regardless of whether the undergraduate belongs to the socially elect or to the majority. There is nothing either extraordinary or novel in this situation. It is an antique arrangement, maintaining itself in the present, and maintaining itself victoriously against perennial challenge. The challenge is called democracy, but the factual equivalent for democracy, particularly in the academic world, is social heterogeneity and intellectual diversification. Harvard, in the heyday of Eliot's presidency, had plausible claim to being such a democracy. It troubled his successor from the beginning, and the latter's whole policy has been aimed at the restoration of social homogeneity and of something akin to intellectual uniformity. Restoration is the correct word. Harvard College was created to be a sectarian academy whose primary purpose was to breed Puritan preachers, and from the outset, through many generations, Harvard kept up a sectarian homogeneity of students and faculty. The inevitable processes of secularization, the

the cultural effect of intermarriage, it cannot be drawn from the facts in hand. Three alternatives are open: the husband is absorbed into the familial *milieu* of his wife, the wife of her husband, or the couple establish a *tertium quid*. In the first two

demands of the new learning in science and in industry, diversified the faculty and dispersed it socially. With the student body, however, the new influences worked otherwise. The homogeneity of "Harvard families" was in no relevant sense broken up. The masses of newcomers became simply a heterogeneous aggregate of individuals among whom the aborigines maintained their associations in superior and unbreached detachment. The sectarian exclusiveness simply got secularized into a no less outstanding social exclusiveness, and the ensuing phenomena were the funny familiar ones of academic snobdom—which begins in certain selected private preparatory schools and terminates in select college clubs. Membership in these clubs was conditioned upon familial relations, mitigated by wealth, by athletic distinction and in very rare instances by distinction in scholarship—the latter being uniformly held as a mark of low caste and worthy only of the greasy grind, who, anyhow, had no business to crowd the gentleman in his own college. So also in other aspects of undergraduate life. Thus, in the class of 1923, the eight major athletic teams had 106 private school men and only 24 from public schools; managers were all private school men, and all the captains, except one. In other activities, including class offices, musical and glee clubs, debating teams and the like, private school men held 112 places to 19 for the public schools. Still other class offices, such as students' councils and "final" clubs, dramatic clubs, class day officers and staff officials on college publications, again went to 183 private school men and 29 to the public school students. On the other hand, although the freshman enrollment of the class showed 316 from private schools and 240 from public schools, of the men who won the highest scholarship honors 82 came from the public schools as against 41 from private schools. In this way the class conflict of the world outside reproduced itself in the college-yard.

In recent years there have been added to the categories of this conflict—rich and poor, well-born and plebeian, gentleman and grind—another pair: native and foreign born. There has been a conspicuous increase in the number of foreign-born students, children of recent immigrants, in American colleges. And of these foreign-born students by far the largest number were Jews. The fact of their being Jews still further multiplied the categories instances the cultural situation remains practically unmodified. The problem is raised by the third in which, if anywhere, the melting-pot would get specification and efficacy. Whether or not it

of class-conflict in undergraduate life, and exacerbated it. It added religious and racial coloring to the social issue. Upon the Jews, prevailingly poor and parvenu, therefore of another class, no less than of another race and religion, class consciousness, class discomforts and class resentments could be easily concentrated. Qualities altogether characteristic of an economic grade could be referred to racial origins and sanctioned by an always active, if sometimes unconscious religious prejudice. And so it was. While the Jews were few in number, inconspicuous therefore, the discrimination against them was equally inconspicuous and lost in the mass of class exclusions. When their numbers grew to noticeable measure, the discrimination grew, and grew in the degree that they developed to the full the traits of the most traditional and approved undergraduate social life—minus, of course, the Back Bay. For in the mass, scholarship was as secondary to them as to their fellow-students. They were as eager to become "real Harvard men" as, in their sermons to freshmen, the president and the deans urged them to. They were eager to mix with their Christian fellows on the much-lauded Harvard terms. They automatically submitted themselves to the completest assimilation possible. And then they found that it takes two to effect an assimilation. Willing as they might be to fuse with the Christians, the Christians wouldn't fuse with them. No clubs, no fraternities, no athletic teams, no association of whatever sort that involved the inward social life of the undergraduate could find any place for them. Willy-nilly, whether as amateur Gentiles or as natural Jews, they were thrown back upon each other for the fellowship of college-life. They created then in their own circle what was refused them when they sought a wider one— the clubs, the fraternities, and such, which are the acme of undergraduate society; and they created them and lived and moved in them in the closest possible imitation of the prevailing approved and emulated traditional type. They assimilated themselves to the Harvard social norm as fully as they were permitted to. They offered it that sincerest flattery of comprehensive imitation; and in so doing they automatically and unwittingly took on the semblance of a new, *un*traditional *un*approved homogeneous familial group, by its mere existence a mockery and a challenge of the approved traditional one.

Of course, the proper sort of undergraduate and professor— those who, in the language of the Hairy Ape, "belonged"—grew scared and disturbed. Harvard, their fair Harvard, was being

does, there is little information, but the opinion
prevails that miscegenated families tend to be unstable ones, inclined to sterility. There is some
anthropological evidence for this opinion; it is,
however, probably far less adequately grounded
than its proponents would have us believe. Even
if the facts were certain, they would not matter,
for the divergent pattern of familial organiza-

invaded by foreigners—and Jews at that. But for a long time
nothing could be done—save as snobbery and innuendo—that
would not lead to the public shame of an exposure of the effective
motives in the anti-Jewish sentiment. After the armistice which
stopped the Great War action became easier and more plausible.
The propaganda of Czarist émigrés, the disseminations of Henry
Ford, the association of Jews with "reds," the fulminations of the
Ku Klux Klan, the veiled, though known and publicly discussed,
limitations upon Jews at Columbia, Princeton, Williams, provided a sympathetic social atmosphere and encouraging academic
precedent. Accusations of moral inferiority were made against
Jews and proved to be false. Then the attack was shifted to the
proposition that beyond a certain proportion—fifteen per cent
precisely—Jews are not assimilable. Anti-Semitic Europe—Hungary, Rumania, Germany, *et al.*—greeted these declarations with
glee, and announced their own practices justified by them. In
America, however, in Harvard College itself, they met great and
unexpected opposition. Public shame came after all. A faculty
committee, appointed to look into the matter of the qualifications
of candidates for entrance to Harvard College, reported unani-
mously in terms which require the old Harvard spirit to be maintained and permit discriminations to be exercised if the administrative officers of the college should choose to do so.

And so the matter stands. The various rationalizations of this
policy offered by Mr. Lowell and his defenders only blacken their
case. For the fact is, that it is not the failure of Jews to be
assimilated into undergraduate society which troubles them.
They do not want them to be assimilated into undergraduate
society. What troubles them is the completeness with which the
Jews have been assimilated. Had they remained dissociated,
unattached, discrete individuals, lost and indistinguishable in the
undergraduate flux, they would have aroused no anxiety. But
they did not so remain. No doubt their taste was bad, and their
standards were undemocratic, but they absorbed as completely as
they were allowed to the associative forms of undergraduate life
which dominate the interests and set the tone of the under-

tion postulated on the stability of the new grouping would only be added to the older ones, parallel
to them, but would not displace them. That such
stable new groupings do take place can be hardly
doubted. That they are desirable as diversifications and enrichments of the plexus of the common life is even less open to doubt. But whether
they shall be diversifications and enrichments is
eventual. Their values come as a function of
their interaction with the rest of the community,
not *a priori*.

The social story, in sum, is the story of both the
persistence and diversification of individual temperament and familial tradition. The persistent
ones get integrated and emphasized in larger
forms of association. Of these the religious has
been the most continuous and the most important.
But all of them have constituted communities
tending to preserve and to sustain the continuity
of the physical stock. Empirically, race is nothing more than this continuity confirmed and enchanneled in basic social inheritances. It is
hardly distinguishable from nationality.

graduate community. Perhaps the merits of these were not dulled
thereby, but their defects were no doubt made the more conspicuous. The action of these assimilating Jews brought into existence
a new familial association which automatically and unconsciously
mocked and challenged the old. The beneficiaries of the latter
felt this and rationalized their feelings, as has been recorded. The
rationalization and its consequences bring into the light of public
discussion a very typical and very amusing example of academic
Know-Nothingism.

VI

As to "democracy":

The confusion about Democracy is greater and more passionate than the confusion about race. Race, when all is said and done, remains an academic conception, a residual issue in the social life of the European peoples of the world. It is invoked as an accessory to the strengthening and justification of other issues which are nearer, more momentous, more "practical." Democracy, however, is itself an issue of practice, invoked in every crisis of economy or politics that arises between the societies which make up the conflict and community of the national life. It is a eulogium applied variously—to an article of political faith, abstract and metaphysically grounded; to an attitude of mind; to a program of reform. It is simultaneously and successively an engine accessory to class struggles; a process of social conflict and readjustment; and a formulary sanctification of the *status quo*. The numerous items to which it is applied are often in fact mutually contradictory and exclusive of one another, according to the efficacious interests they conceal or propound. But they all have the same ideological root which is laid bare whenever some protagonist of democracy, crowded in argument, feels himself against the ropes. This root is the conception of

man that was current among the reformers and
political theorists of the eighteenth century. It is
the doctrine of the "natural man" with his "natural rights," entering as a free agent into a free
contract with his utter equals, and so creating society—as modern states are supposed to have created the League of Nations—by unanimous consent.

Now this doctrine enables the interests concerned to sanctify both the equalities and the in-
equities of modern societies. Consider just one
example. There is that central and very complicated and peculiar institution of our society
called private property—much involved in the
current fear of the alien. About the control of
this institution the classes of the community have
been carrying on an ever more passionate battle.
There are those who want to abolish it as the chief
enemy of man, and there are those who want to
preserve it as the chief friend of man. Both invoke the eulogium of democracy for their desires.
Property, say the communists, superimposes artificial differences upon the natural equality of
men; it shifts the incidence of value from the
labor power, the inherent energies which constitute personality, to things which need have no
dynamic origin in the personality at all. It substitutes possessions for life, property rights for
human rights. By pooling property, the balance

of society will be redressed; the condition of the
original social contract, which was a pooling of
wills, will be restored; classes will disappear; men
will be free men again because equal men. And
freedom and equality are what democracy consists of. Property, say the capitalists, is the visi,
ble symbol of social equality. A man's personal,
ity does not end at his skin, but extends outward
to everything that he needs and produces. To
take away his property is like slicing him off because he is fat, or cutting his legs because he is
tall. The equality of men lies in the fact of their
existence, not in the manner of their existence,
Property is as inevitable in it as fatness or tall,
ness. It is the external expression of the inner
qualities of the individual. It is what, under the
social contract, a man's fellows bind themselves
impartially to keep secure for him. And this is
the essence of democracy. Property is the ward
of democracy, its symbol and palladium.

And there you are. Any of the particular ob-
jectives that a special pleader may be aiming at
will be defended in an elaborate dialectic of which
democracy is the conclusion. Prohibition or personal freedom, the draft or voluntary enlistment,
capitalism or socialism, the closed shop or the
open—the dialectic is applied with equal success
to all. Unfortunately, nothing can be made
from such talk. Democracy is an afterthought

in it, designed to set the sanction of respectability upon ends felt to be questionable or subject to opposition. In the language of the "new" psychology, it is a rationalization for the privileged and a compensation for the disinherited.

Outside of the uses of democracy, its positive substance consists of certain continuous and expanding practices in the behavior of man. Whatever logical form or dialectical pattern the statement of these practices might fall into, their significance as living facts lies in the constant impact, disintegration and readjustment of old customs, old traditions, old standards with the new knowledge, new machines, new wealth and new habits. The democracy which is an existing quality of society is neither static nor structural. These by their very nature cannot enter into democracy. The democracy which is an existing quality of society consists first of all in the mutual compenetration of the old with the new, the dissolution of each by the other. Secondly, it consists of the tendency or direction of this compenetration in time and in people. It is for these that the formulæ of its philosophers and chieftains set, in so far as they are truly expressive, the logical limits.

These formulæ may be summed up in what Sir Henry Maine once signalized as the transition from status to contract. Status is that which at bottom is implied in the given relationships of the familial community. It appears in the patriarchal order of ancient society, where the relative positions of the housefather, the housemother, and the children are fixed and inalterable throughout their lives. There the familial edifice and the system of habits it comprehends are developments, elaborations, exaggerations or refinements of the biological relationships. These relationships are what the logicians call *internal*. They are integral to the individual's existence. They cannot be destroyed without at the same time destroying the individuals whom they bind into a group. This group, which is usually called the "family," has an obscurely organic character. Its existence is inevitable, and it is always implicit in other forms of grouping and cuts across them. People cannot cease to be sons or daughters, or parents, or cousins or grandparents without ceasing to be. The relationships impose, among the individuals they bind, a priority of claim on each other's attention and regard which society acknowledges, and against which it sets very few superior claims and those only in times of danger to the whole community.

All these relationships are relationships of status. One does not acquire them, one is born into them and their implications carry over directly from their biological springs into the customs and stations of the community. The family, the tribe, the caste, the nationality, the church, the guild, the state, were all, at one time or another, a projection of biological relationships into non-biological groupings; hereditary associations, into every one of which, it was supposed, men were born; within which all had predestined stations. The history of freedom, of the expansion of democracy, has been largely and broadly the tale of how this rigid, involuntary, predestined status has been getting replaced by voluntary contract, and free association has superseded involuntary. The degree of change has, of course, varied with time, and place, and circumstance; so also have the alterations of the institutional pattern in which the changes are registered; so has the range of their application. Occidental society is just in the process of applying them in any appreciable or significant way to women; and only among philosophers, and among very occasional idealistic laymen, is there any idea of including children within their scope. They became operative with respect to the Church only at the end of the Wars of the Reformation; to the guilds, with the beginning of industrial capitalism; to the State, toward the end of the nineteenth century.

The elimination of the relationship of status from these fields of human association is, however, only the negative side of the story. Its complementary positive aspect is the multifold diversification of groupings, and the incorporation of the idea of their contractual nature into the commonsense of the western world. The relationship into which a person enters when he enters any one of them is recognized as an *external* relationship. He is not born with it, he acquires it and the group which it defines can be destroyed without destroying him or his fellows who compose it. The group is an *organization,* its existence as a whole is dependent upon and derives from the existence of its parts, whereas the group based on *internal* relationships is an organism, the existence of the parts depending upon and deriving from the existence of the whole. The members of organizations can exist without them, can join them and leave them at will; the members of an organism lack both these advantages. They are in the whole and of the whole, and their relationships to it and one another are fixed and inalterable; relationships of status. States, nations, churches, colleges, parties, fraternal orders, clubs, professions, crafts, armies, navies, legislatures, and so on, world without end, are organizations. Membership in them is voluntary. One is —according to preference or need—now a citizen of the United States, then of Great Britain; now a member of a Chamber of Commerce, then of a labor union; now a physician, then a carpenter; now a Baptist, then an Episcopalian; now an Elk, then an Odd Fellow; now a Republican, then a Democrat; now a soldier, then a sailor. And so on indefinitely. Membership may be put on and laid off, in many groups at once or in few, or in none. It is a voluntary association, based on consent, open to alternatives. One's line of ancestry and familial connections admit of no alternatives. They are fate, not choice, and the struggle for freedom has been not a little the endeavor to resist, to neutralize the dominion of this fate. Democracy has meant the multiplication of the contractual relations; it has consisted in the formation, clash, integration, dissolution and reformation of ever more and more associations wherewith the individual may give his life purpose, import, color and direction; it has been identical with the manifold growth and diversification of groupings that serve as engines of lability and liberation for the individual. For this reason it has also been identical with a social life less assured, fuller of problems and alternatives, rich in symbiotic forms of corruption and evil, more necessitous of the uses of knowledge and the ways of intelligence. Democracy has meant, literally, not government of the people, by the people, for the people, but freedom of association of the people, among the people, with the people.

Now both the dissolution of the institutions based on status and the passions of class conflicts rationalized on the ground of race differences have blinded the protagonists of democracy to the just claim which these differences have to the same freedom of associative life demanded for other types. Empirically, the familial community with its elaboration in the qualities of nationality is, even if we disregard its primary and indissoluble character, at least one fact of grouping among the other facts. In the give and take between groups which is the life of society its beneficences are at least as conspicuous as its maleficence. The latter has, on the whole, been distinctly checked by the democratic movement, though the chaos in Central Europe shows that the capacity for evil is still the immortal twin of the potentiality for good. All existence is morally neutral, and what it generates either of excellence or turpitude lies rather in its relations with its neighbors than in any quality in itself. Too often, the repression of turpitude carries with it the frustration of excellence. In the case of nationality this has conspicuously been so. Historically and logically democracy is not the enemy but the partner of nationality. Nationality wedded to democracy can never become imperialism of any kind; democracy paced by nationality can never become the anarchy of association that it lies within its nature to be. In the joining of the two, nationality becomes simply another among the modes of association with his fellows in which the individual lives and moves and has his being. Familial in its essence, it seems to function largely as the social area of individual reference, the field where the tension, crisis, and resolution of the adjustments between the individual and other individuals and associations are registered and signalized. For, being the efficacious natural *milieu* or habitat of his temperament, it enters more than any other mode of association into each of his relationships with the residual community. It is the center at which he stands, the point of his most intimate social reactions, therefore of his intensest emotional life. When he is free, he is free because this flows unrepressed and unobstructed into integration with the other relationships whereby his hyphenated existence is constituted. He is then an unmuted instrument in the orchestra of civilization. His tone is full and clear. The unique timbre of his personality enters actively and positively into the necessary social diversity which cannot be a diversity of individuals without being simultaneously and coimplicatively a diversity of natural, organic groups. Lacking these, democracy is frustrated; supplemented by them, it becomes creative. As Mr. Norman Hapgood says: "It would be far better

for the richness and value of existence if in diverse ways we could all have devotion to certain,
rich specific ideals of our own, to those which we
are particularly fitted to carry out." If any gift
of particular fitness, begged, unearned, lies anywhere in an individual or an association, it lies
there, in the natural or ethnic group. That imparts to it its first impulse, its characteristic
skill, and its spontaneous direction. All else is
acquired. The significance of democracy for
these and of these for democracy is patent.

VII

Finally, as to "culture":

It is a commonplace among psychologists that
the intrinsic qualities of human beings are likely
to show themselves most unmixed in those of their
activities into which regard for the environment
and for organic needs enters least. In such activities the races of men are most nearly autonomous
and free. What they perform is an utterance and
communication of themselves, not an adjustment
to the environment. It is a spontaneous play,
like a bird singing or a dog baying at the moon,
a genuine revelation of their genius, a reliable
prophecy of its import. It is the fine, as contrasted with the industrial arts, and its various
skills and disciplines have been held almost uni-

versally as the paramount constituents of culture and the infallible gauge of civilization among any people, of any clime or time. That this enthronement of them involves a gross injustice; that it is a prejudice transmitted from the days when the industrial arts were the arts practiced only by the slaves and the rabble, and the fine arts were the arts only of the aristocrats and the masters; that the former were degraded through force and the latter exalted by parasitism, does not militate against the psychological commonplace. Even the industrial arts eventuate in non-utilitarian, inefficacious end-forms of both tools and products; in pure decorative quality, supervening on use and crowning it; forms not necessary, simply the final steps in an execution inwardly prompted and satisfying predilections of eye, ear and hand. Architecture is the pivotal example of this relationship though it obtains in all of the industrial arts. In a certain sense, the decorative end-forms that complete instrumental and functional structure are more truly revelatory than the forms of the fine arts as such. They bespeak the group temperament emerging through the utilities and coming free of them. The critical tradition which seeks to understand national genius and to interpret national character by the state of its fine arts, then, grasps at a half-truth, but is not unwise.

In the United States critical wisdom has always been moved less by judgment than by anxiety and aspiration. Consciousness of deficiency in music, painting, sculpture, architecture and literature, particularly literature, has been a persistent trait of the American mind from the time the British colonies defended themselves as the American nation. Prior to that time their esthetic sentiment and cultural outlook had been acquiescently British and colonial. Their elaborations and refinements of life had been importations from England; their original ideas and reflections, adaptations from France. Their traditional thinking followed the patterns set by Calvinistic theology. Their spontaneous thinking centered upon politics and adapted the forms of French thought to colonial needs. Significantly, it was far more original with the landlords of the South than with the merchants of the North: the kinship of even Hamilton is in birth and background nearer to Virginia than to Massachusetts. But the adoption of the Constitution put a period to original political thinking. The successors of Hamilton and Jefferson only perpetuated a tradition, a tradition which found its terminal in the Civil War. They were concerned far more with the interpretation of the Constitution than with the analysis and resolution of the political problem. Colonialism in political thought ceased, only to be replaced by legalism. The political premises went unquestioned; issues came to crisis only about their implications. Political thinking ceased to be reflection and became scholasticism with the Supreme Court in the rôle of the Benedictines and Franciscans, and the Constitution for a Summa Theologiæ.

Hope was strong that the declaration of political independence which was consummated by the acknowledgment of the British colonies as free and sovereign states would have further consummation in esthetic and cultural sovereignty. Aspiring patriots hungered for independence and freedom in the spiritual life. Culturally, America was to be an autonomous creative whole, self-sufficient and self-sufficing, with its own sovereign painting, sculpture, architecture, music and literature, literature particularly, the peer of any, with a claim equal to any on international recognition and regard. That these did not exist was acknowledged, but the sense of cultural inferiority and the feeling of esthetic insufficiency was more than compensated for by the cultural hope. Of course the United States was a raw country, of course it was a young country, undeveloped, unadorned. Was it not also, however, a free country, and a good country, with an empty past, and therefore, inevitably, a uniquely noble future? Sooner or later, probably sooner, the great American artist would appear, to captivate and astound. Irving, Poe, Emerson, Whitman, Howells, and their literary descendants of this day and generation issued the same challenge and uttered the same prophecy. They called many, and never a one was chosen. Whitman's "literatus" is still a hope deferred, and that hope deferred turns to despair is not a maxim for nothing. It is exemplified in at least the yearning distress of the "younger intellectuals."

Also eager and declarant of literary and cultural independence, and more so, than their forbears, the young ones cry aloud that the young country and the good country and the free country has failed to keep its promise. It has produced pigs instead of poets, machines and money instead of men, bunk instead of beauty. It is a country evangelical, superficial, afraid of ideas, gullible and smart; starved in its intellectual and esthetic life, coarse in its pleasures, vulgar in its tastes, surrendering all things pertaining to the spirit into the hands of the female of the species. Of its artists it makes merchants, of its thinkers, preachers. Demanding, above all, conformity, it stifles genius and prostitutes talent. How, unendowed with an autonomous cultural past, can it have a cultural future? It is still merely colonial, "an English colonial possession," says

Mr. Mencken, "intellectually and spiritually." The American author who would be American is, staying at home, condemned to "a sort of social and intellectual vacuum"; if he would find comradeship, he must wander. "Whenever one encounters a novel that rises superior . . . the thing takes on a subtle but unmistakable air of foreignness . . . in part grounded soundly enough on the facts. The native author of any genuine force and originality is almost invariably found to be under strong foreign influences, either English or Continental. It was so in the earliest days. Freneau, the poet of the Revolution, was thoroughly French in blood and traditions. Irving, as H. R. Haweis has said, 'took to England as a duck takes to water,' and was in exile seventeen years. Cooper, with the great success of *The Last of the Mohicans* behind him, left the country in disgust and was gone for seven years. Emerson, Bryant, Lowell, Hawthorne, and even Longfellow kept their eyes turned across the water; Emerson, in fact, was little more than an importer and popularizer of German and French ideas. Bancroft studied in Germany; Prescott, like Irving, was enchanted by Spain. Poe, unable to follow the fashion, invented mythical travels to save his face—to France, to Germany, to the Greek Isles. The

Civil War revived the national consciousness enormously, but it did not halt the movement of the émigrés. Henry James, in the seventies, went to England, Bierce and Bret Harte followed him, and even Mark Twain, absolutely American though he was, was forever pulling up stakes and setting out for Vienna, Florence and London. Only poverty tied Whitman to the soil; his audience, for many years, was chiefly beyond the water, and there, too, he often longed to be. This distaste for the national scene is often based upon a genuine alienness. The more, indeed, one investigates the ancestry of Americans who have won distinction in the fine arts, the more one discovers tempting game for the critical Know-Nothings. Whitman was half Dutch, Harte was half Jew, Poe was partly German, James had an Irish grandfather, Howells was largely Irish and German, Dreiser is German, and Hergesheimer is Pennsylvania Dutch. Fully a half of the painters discussed in John C. Van Dyke's *American Painting and Its Tradition* were of mixed blood, with the Anglo-Saxon plainly recessive. And of the five poets singled out for encomium by Miss Lowell in *Tendencies in Modern American Poetry* one is a Swede, two are partly German, one was educated in the German language, and three of the

five exiled themselves to England as soon as they
got out of their nonage.   The exiles are of all
sorts: Frank Harris, Vincent O'Sullivan, Ezra
Pound, Herman Scheffauer, T. S. Eliot, Henry
B. Fuller, Stuart Merrill, Edith Wharton.
They go to England, France, Germany, Italy—
anywhere to escape.   Even at home the literatus
is perceptibly foreign in his mien.   If he lies
under the New England tradition he is furiously
colonial—more English than the English.   If
he turns to revolt, he is apt to put on a French
hat and a Russian red blouse. . . . This tendency of American literature, the moment it begins to show enterprise, novelty and significance,
to radiate a foreign smell is not an isolated phenomenon. . . . Whenever one hears that a new
political theory is in circulation, or a scientific
heresy, or a movement toward rationalism in religion, it is safe to guess that some discontented
stranger or other has a hand in it . . . intellectual experimentation is chiefly left to immigrants
of the later migrations, and the small sections of
the native population that have been enriched
with their blood. . . . All the arts in America
are thoroughly exotic.   Music is almost wholly
German or Italian, painting is French, architecture . . . is a maddening phantasmagoria of
borrowings. . . ." [1]   In sum, the United States

[1] H. L. Mencken: *Prejudices,* Second Series, pp. 44 *seq.*

is culturally naked, wearing an esthetic barrel of foreign make. We are a comfortable, but not a cultivated community.

Need it be pointed out that it is the intellectual attitude, not the facts toward which the attitude is taken that is the cause of the despair? What literature has not had its exiles and lonely souls, or otherwise come under foreign influence? Of how many artists can it be said that their blood is pure? All that Mr. Mencken's rhodomontade attests is that creation comes from the impact of diversities, a truism which nobody will deny. Mr. Mencken converts the truism into an indictment because he is a romantic protestant, a reactionary Utopian. His theory of life and letters requires that culture shall be sustained by a "civilized aristocracy, secure in its position, animated by an intelligent curiosity, skeptical of all facile generalizations, superior to the sentimentality of the mob, and delighting in the battle of ideas for its own sake." Such an aristocracy is, like Plato's philosopher-king, a figment of its author's imagination. It has no ground either in psychology or in history. The qualities of mind it is to be endowed with have never been a function of security but of insecurity, and of insecurity in the presence of whatever aristocracy there happened to be challenging them. Vested interests of the body invest the mind with their own partizanship, as the history of aristocracies shows. The play and progress of ideas have been the outcome of other conflicts than those of ideas, and their future has been contingent upon the clash of classes, the confrontation of communities,[1] the free association and collaboration of thereby uprooted individuals coming out of all kinds of corporate unities into a sort of no-class land where the distinction between lord and yokel is obliterated and the distinction between master-craftsman and amateur becomes coercive. From Plato to Darwin and beyond, this has been the case, and the recorded rôle of aristocracies in this stretch of intellectual and cultural history is a complete repudiation of Mr. Mencken's ideal so far as it purports to derive from the facts in the case. Where these are concerned, this brave and well-read critic does not seem to know what he is talking about.

Cultural values arise upon the confrontation, impact, and consequent disintegration and readjustment of different orders, with the emergence therefrom of new harmonies carrying unprecedented things in their heart. They have not had a different origin in the United States, as Mr. Mencken attests, nor are their future springs likely to be of a different kind. Their quality

[1] Cf. Petrie: *The Revolutions of Civilization:* "Every civilization of a settled population tends to incessant decay from its maximum position. . . ."

will necessarily vary with the variety, pitch and timbre of the forces whose interplay and reverberation they so largely are. The cultural prospect can be indicated in the cultural retrospect, although it cannot, so changeful is the constellation of influences in the American scene, be predicted.

The story of America's spiritual past is easily told. It is the story of the accommodation of a sad and deeply moralized people to a wilderness. It is the tragedy of a morality at war with a vacuum, wherein the morality has been transformed from an order and discipline of living into a compensatory check upon life. For the devastating fact regarding the American continent which has become the domicile of the American peoples was that it was empty and pure, unmarked, unconverted by the hand of man. The Indians do not signify. Their society was an adjustment to the exigencies of nature, not a resistance against them, nor a conquest over them. Their being and passing left no traces; a season's change, and their dwelling places were wilderness again. Nature, then, in North America, was untamed. The scene remained windswept and sunburnt, never kept. In contrast, Europe, particularly the Europe from which the first settlers came, was to America as a house to a moor. There the hands of man had been at

work for uncounted millennia; his works overlaid
the scene in strata, imparting to it a contour,
content and atmosphere into which the life of
the generations is continuously interwoven, which
was so immemorially implied in custom, tradition
and habit that there could hardly be an open
without guideposts, a new problem without ancestral solutions, a quarrel without rules for its
conduct and laws for its settlement.   No novelty
could be quite new, no discovery quite sudden.
Change, in Europe, built upon these massive
material and spiritual survivals from the past,
was continuous with them, and in certain clear
and inexpugnable ways limited by them.   Neither
the cataclysms of nature nor the revolutions of
man could eradicate them.   Indeed, if the story
of revolution is veridical, they were never so coercive as when men were in rebellion against
them.   They are the substance of continuity in
the life of man on European soil.

American soil held no parallel for them.   The
companies of white men who made it their habitation brought with them from Europe the social
arrangement which implied Europe, not America: memories, beliefs, customs, traditions, skills,
and a certain amount of material and tools upon
which the skills particularly were conditioned.
The residual conditions, the massive humanized
natural *milieu,* the physical bodies of the com-

munity's institutional life, the residual population and its associative patterns, they could not
bring over. But their skills and habits were adjustments to all of these, and without them were
like activities carried on in a vacuum. They
moved as men might move from under whose
feet the ground had fallen, yet were unaware.
The consequences were of the sort that dislocation always brings. Small bands in an unknown
wilderness, with a living difficult to get and precarious to keep, they fell into fear. Fear imparted a poignant preciousness to the conditions of security to which their lives had been
attuned and which were no longer theirs. Fear
made every stranger suspect and all otherness
guilt. Fear peopled the wilderness with its customary incarnations—devils, ogres, witches; and
fear planted them in the very hearts of the
neighbors. So the settlers killed Indians, persecuted religious dissidents, tortured and murdered
old women and young for witchcraft, exorcised
the devil and invoked God with an intensity of
fear that only prosperity and the filling of the
scene with fellow men could relax, and finally
did relax. Fear was relaxed but not destroyed.
For prosperity came slowly and came arduously
and came as the result of habituation in a new
way of life, of a new complexus of customs and
skills evoked by the natural environment and

adjusted to its exigencies. In part a learning from the Indians, in part the outcome of bitter and toilful experimentation with the natural scene, this new organization had for its foci the cultivation of maize and the hunting of game. A certain dubious nomadism is a part of it, and a brave, free, practical facility. Its upshot and integration are the temperament of the pioneer.

The qualities of this temperament have been much discussed. Many virtues have been attributed to it, and not a few vices. Evaluations of it have, however, been prevailingly moral and political, not psychological. And for this reason its cultural significance has been completely missed. For the pioneer is not a simple primitive in a primitive land. The pioneer is a civilized personality rendered primitive by the necessities of his environment, a collective Robinson Crusoe without the literary providence of his author's amenities. His nature retains the marks of both his conditions and origins. By virtue of them it attains a duplexity of another denomination than any among the common European hypocrisies. It is not at all a hypocrisy in the usual sense of the term. It is a genuine fission and folding over of life, a duplexity, without being a dissociation. That is, the duplex temperament is not a disintegrated one; it has unity and direction. It is conscious of both aspects of its behavior, but it is

not conscious of any contradiction or strain between them. When they come to consciousness
they are called conscience, and it is only among
the groups that have ceased to be pioneer that
this happens and a habit of conscience, like the
"New England conscience," becomes institutional. Strain and contradiction are ends, not
beginnings. The urge which they split is the
same urge, bifurcated by the different materials
that enchannel it. Had these materials been on
the same qualitative plane of existence, making
homologous demands and exercising the same
compulsions upon personality, they would have
installed a genuine hypocrisy. They exist, however, and operate, upon different levels in different dimensions. One is the coercive matter of
the natural scene from which men must win their
livings at the risk of their lives; with which, consequently, men must willy-nilly make fruitful
conjunctions that get established in habit and
solidified in custom—custom and habit of individual effort, self-dependence, resourcefulness
and daring, recklessness and lawlessness; all in
all, the spirit of Jurgen, ready to try anything
once, at his own risk.

The other is the imported behavior-pattern of
the community life, with its memories, folkways,
habits and traditions, all adjustment to an environment that they are now no longer in the

presence of, and consequently dislocated, irrelevant, therefore dammed and in frustration. Instead of being channels of energy leading into the environment, they have become, like unused roads that turn to swamps, reservoirs of emotion, moral cul-de-sacs, whence impulse flows back into the organism and effort recoils upon itself. That this sort of check upon activity sometimes brings madness is a commonplace, and there is a persistent legend regarding a pathological strain in Puritanism. More often, however, the check brings an intense imaginative life in which the conditions and objects of the blocked and dislocated habits become in a fresh way insurance in fantasy against the insecurities of fact. They become the present concretions of the vestigial past. Replaced without being destroyed by the new habits of community, thrust by them simply into the secondary, desuetudinous, thinner, superficial level of life, they survive there as symbols and images of a lapsed but remembered good, sanctions for the endurance of present evil and assurances of escape from it. Instead of being distributed over all the institutions of the community, they generally become focalized in one. In this one the continuity of the pioneer present with the civilized past is incarnated and signalized; the reminiscence of European standards is preserved, the release of the pioneer's emotions from the compulsion of the immediate and from relevancy to the thing in hand is effectuated. The institution is the Church. The engines and agencies of its cultus, its Book, its communions, its revivals and its preachments become, at one and the same time, recollection of the past, present security, future fortune, in a world of chance and risk and darkness. The pioneer is thus a Puritan compelled to live in the primitive present; the Puritan is the pioneer, remembering the civilized past. The two are functions of one another, and grow and diminish together.

They have grown by misfortune, they have diminished in prosperity. Inevitably, much of the story of the frontier is the story of their growth. For the westward march of the white man across the North American continent has been a march farther and farther from the base of cultural supply, a thinning and attrition of the original complex inheritance of culture to the final simple one of cultus. The degree and speed of recovery may be measured by the degree of nearness to the seaboard, and to the possibility of diverse contacts and other avenues of emotional release, except where, as in California, climate was too much for conscience, and the Puritan became the playboy of the western world. Thus, the first scene of cultural recovery was the scene where the pioneer started and the cultural attrition began. It was New England; and it was New England that had been the first to attain a widely distributed prosperity which enabled the importation of foreign patterns for new channels of the emotional life. The enrichment of this life in art and letters is the most significant contribution to American culture made by the New England school. For this reason it was in New England, if anywhere, that the practice of the arts of life caught up with its compensations and preachments, and the duplexity approached a harmony. The Calvinistic bitterness of the compensatory memory was replaced by a generalized good will: Cotton Mather came to fruition in Channing, Jonathan Edwards in Emerson. If the intellectual and passional quality of these and their fellowship of poets, novelists, painters and historians was not of the very first order, it was, nevertheless, of an order high and spacious; if it was largely a contagion from Europe, it was even more an expansion of life into more gracious, more liberal and happier forms. It became a measure and a palladium for the westward states which, otherwise isolated, would never in other ways have been freed to look beyond the non-conformist church for the utterance of the whole spirit of man.

Much of the generation which came to fruition in this expanded way was born before the thirties of the last century. Its youth rebelled against the unspeakable Mexican War; its maturity directed the Civil War; its old age guided the industrial exploitation of the continent in field and forest and mine, through road and factory. Its last survivor is scarcely dead in Henry Adams, whose word, being its last word, is something of a cry of despair over the havoc his compeers wrought, winning the west to industry.

What, without the new economy of industry, might have been the cultural story of these United States, is matter for the speculative poet. This economy is a terrific fact; industry is a going concern which drives agriculture and the pioneer of the agricultural economy before it. With it have come other facts, of which the most important is that industry keeps the United States a country of pioneers. Of pioneers with, however, a difference. The westward course of the white men from Europe across the North American continent continues. But it is no longer a course into an unknown wilderness. It is no longer the highway of a progressive separation from the borderline of civilization. Free land in the United States came practically to an end with the beginning of the 20th century. By that time there was no area of possible habitation worth mentioning which was not in some

way privately enclosed. Much had gone into the
hands of railroads as the reward of virtue in
business enterprise; much had been absorbed by
speculators and promoters. The residue was
the possession of an agricultural population,
densest in the Mississippi Valley, whose pioneer
habits had hardened into a sort of second nature
under the conditions of enforced settlement. It
was this population that was to be the source of
profit and the theme of exploitation to the industrial captains. It was no longer the homogeneous population of the Puritan age. From
1848 onwards, it had served as the nucleus of accretion for immigrants from Germany and Scan-
dinavia, immigrants of another speech and another heritage than the British, undergoing the
reconstruction of pioneership in reaction not
merely to primeval Nature undefiled, but in reaction also to a constellation of community life
alien to their own in pattern, content and implication. Later came what Mr. Santayana calls
the miscellany of Europe—Irish, Jews, Italians,
Magyars, Slavs, Spaniards, and so on; a few to
take up land, most to serve the industrial machine according to their need and its advantage.
The exigencies of the machine were added to and
then began to displace the exigencies of the land.
Cities grew and multiplied. The "white collar"
proletarian, the desk and counter workers, who

are bourgeois spirits with proletarian bodies, the clerks, the salespersons, the advertisers, the journalists, all the new diversified horde of city-dwelling economic middlemen, multiplying more rapidly than any other section of the population, became, by their mere mass and unhappiness, a strong urban reduplication of the pioneer duplexity. For the immigrants, the exigencies of this complicated and duplex native habit of life were an addition to the exigencies of the land and the machine. Everywhere, community confronted and made impact upon community; everywhere, consequently, dislocation of custom, disintegration of habit, confusion of conduct, perplexity of mind. And through all, relentless, inescapable, the unyielding patterns of industrial behavior set by the machine for farmer no less than for worker; the static formulæ of political doctrine set by the law of a bygone time; the implicit and overt conflicts between the two.

The generations during whose lifetime this mêlée was coming to consciousness were the generations whose conscious standards derived from the New England enlightenment. They were the generations that brought into being and developed the numberless small sectarian colleges and the few great public universities of the Middle West and beyond, and filled them with professors from the New England schools. They

were the generations that built Chicago and the
great coastal and riparian cities of the Lake region and the Mississippi Valley. They were the
generations whose next turn it was, after New
England, to come to prosperity and order and
so to leisure and culture. The land which their
life civilized was the land in which the ethnic diversification was least confused; where British,
Germans, Scandinavians, and Slavs, were most
definitely concentrated in their own communities
and least obscured in their ways of life.

The first phase of Middle Western culture
was radically different from the New England
first phase. Its soil was not foreign commerce
and manufacture; its soil was packing and iron-
mongering. It was not a transplantation from
Europe; it was a graft from New England. It
was an absorption and transmutation of the
sweetness and light of that stern and rockbound
coast into the ways and substance of the cam-
pestrian life of the Middle West. The liberal
expansion of this life was consequently not so
great nor so diversified as that accomplished a
generation before by New England through its
discovery of Europe. The old focalization of
cultural tradition in the cultus was too little disturbed. The compenetration of the two was inadequate. Prosperity failed, hence, to flower in
a more gracious and beautiful life. It became

rather a device for reproducing itself. "Culture" was understood, not as a way of life, but as a decoration of the liver, a sort of independent variable which might be put on and laid off like a garment; it was held as the decent clothing of the rich—and their habit was to dress their wives better than themselves. Intellectual and emotional interest took divergent directions—the one along the line of the humane precedent set by New England; the other, in continuation of the tradition of the church. The confrontation of the two could not, however, fail to be fruitful. These Main Streets of the spirit were bound at points to cross and clash, as cross and clash they did. They were bound at other points to become implicated by impact and compenetration with the hard adventures of industrial exploitation and financial oppression to which the whole Mississippi Valley was then conspicuously subject, and they were. But so being and doing, they brought vision and judgment. The insurgence of Progressivism and the awakening of the literary imagination were contemporary. From Eugene Field to Frank Norris, from Frank Norris to Booth Tarkington, from Booth Tarkington to Sherwood Anderson and all their fellows and contemporaries and all between; from Indianapolis to Chicago, from Chicago to St. Louis, they have brought vision and judgment.

It is a bitterer vision, a less romantic judgment, than that of the New England School. But so are the life and labor of man more bitter, the clash and cumber of habits sharper, the confrontation and dissolution and re-creation of values more swift and more true. More forces are involved, and more diversified forces. The social background has an ethnic plaiting New England knew not of; the cultural foreground a clash of classes New England could not anticipate. Frank Norris and Hamlin Garland; Theodore Dreiser and Booth Tarkington, Sinclair Lewis and Sherwood Anderson; Henry Webster and Edna Ferber; Upton Sinclair and Robert Herrick; Edgar Masters and Carl Sandburg—they are all raw, less artists than prophets, all showing the absence of a steady discipline of workmanship which only the enduring custom and sustaining tradition of locality and community can generate.

If there is an exception, it is Vachel Lindsay. In him village and field, church and road and country-store, their rhythms and legends, their fears and ardors, are liberated and come to beauty. The folk life, the folk memory and the folk hope, with its cadences from the non-conformist hymnal and its African modulations, in which the whole valley finds its nearest freedoms, Lindsay integrates and utters. He

speaks more nearly for the soul of Puritan-pio-
neer America than any other. Is it without
significance that he is not held in high regard yet?

His art is of a simplicity too unsophisticated,
too clear, too obvious and too traditional; too
fresh a repristination of the past, and too near
the meeting house on the Main Street and the
State Road leading out of it, for a complex and
troubled generation of mere intellectuals of urban habits. Its localism of spirit and rhythm
has a centrality on either side of which resound
the no less local but much more intellectualized
timbres of Robert Frost and Edwin Robinson
and Conrad Aiken; of James Oppenheim and
Louis Untermeyer and Maxwell Bodenheim; of
H. D. and Amy Lowell and James Cabell; of
Carl Sandburg and Alfred Kreymborg and Edgar Masters. Poetry has the spontaneous localism, the responsiveness to the intimacies of community, caste and class which the other disciplines seem to lack, and without which the workmanship necessary to turn the noblest or most
enticing matter into the substance and form of
art does not seem to eventuate. In poetry race,
locality and cultural atmosphere work out more
obviously than in prose into beautiful patterns of
sound and meaning, and it is to poetry that the
enrichment from these diversities has first ac-
crued. It is poetry that is called the best and

most vigorous of the fine arts practiced in the United States to-day. In poetry the cultural promise of the non-British enclaves is conspicuously made. Out of their fusion of geographic localism and cultural nationality, with its solid and sustained rhythm and timbre of attitude and feeling, the poets enter into the national letters, and they are the more national in the degree that they attain to the perfect utterance of their race and place.

The sort of social and political challenge these racialized localities make to American life has already been noted.[1] Need it now be added that their most significant contribution is cultural? It is through no accident that Mr. Mencken is able to signalize so many persons of mixed or non-British blood and familial background as the light and leading of the American mind in science, in letters, in the graphic arts; even as it is through no accident that American artists of native ancestry speak of America through foreign inspiration. Imagination and understanding, when they are creative and not purely compensations or rationalizations, are the fruits of conflict, devoted to reconciliation. They are the

[1] I do not discuss the influence of the negro upon the esthetic material and cultural character of the South and the rest of the United States. This is at once too considerable and too recondite in its processes for casual mention. It requires a separate analysis.

harmonies that supervene upon the crossing of ways of life and ways of thought, the security which reflection wins from the insecurity of action. It has been characteristic of pioneer conditions that this security should be reverenced as a memory of the past rather than employed as a mastering of the present, that it should be religion's consolation against the workday's perils. And it has been ever so, where men faced nature bare of hand, and perhaps will ever be so. Now the pioneering of fact has come to its period: men no longer need to win from the wilderness a living barehanded. Nature in these United States has been tamed and harnessed up. The problem of nature has lapsed. Its place has been taken by the problem of man. The challenge of things is superseded by the challenge of personality, the struggle of ideals.

Authority has it that the times current are a pivotal field, a critical phase in the procession of this new American struggle. Once more men sit in judgment upon their own works; once more the drift of circumstance becomes subject for wide analysis and planned redirection. The evidences of it are cheap, even, if you wish it so, vulgar; but they truly speak for an urge toward understanding and mastery. Business, which used to be a gamble, seeks to become a profession. It replaces reliance on shrewdness with reliance on statistics. Labor unions and banking houses create their especial "research divisions." The schools and colleges organize departments of business administration and award degrees in business proficiency. Of course, such things are not "cultural" in the traditional sense of this term. Neither was science, in its beginnings; neither is science now, to a large section of the community which, brought up in the tradition of the academic *trivium* and *quadrivium,* can see no other stuff to humanistic life than those dead things. But culture is no such dead thing. It ensues wherever public habit has been translumined by a sentiment aware of its ground, direction and implications; wherever uses have been refined to beauty, wherever a harmony has been consciously established between the forms and functions of things. All societies have their appropriate excellences, according to the institutions into which they are patterned, the material channels through which their energies come to freedom and to form. It is not written in the stars that industrial society can evade this felicity, and fail of its own unique excellence. With its future pattern implicit in its present structure, the relation of the two can be studied in their minutiæ and worked out from next to next as a man grows, not as a thing is fabricated. It is upon this relation, relevantly, and not as bub-

bles in the blue, that ideas come into play, and
out of it only that a pertinent and noble culture
can exfoliate. Everything else is escape, in root
and attitude and value not less retrospective and
reactionary than the Puritanism which it con-
tradicts. Mostly rebellion and compensation,
this residual Cult of Culture elaborates no implications of the going life into beauty; loves the
good far less than it hates what it calls bad. It
simply opposes the secular tradition of letters
to the clerical, and the enduring part of it derives not from its rebellions or its compensatory
idealizations, but from the affirmative appreciations which it absorbs from the sciences of things
and of man that are coming more and more to be
the tonic notes in the composition of communal
life.

It is within the unifying, all-enveloping atmosphere of science and industry that a man
to-day must come to himself. Against the architectonic and regimentation of the latter, the logical oneness of the former, the deep-lying cultural
diversities of the ethnic groups are the strongest
shield, the chief defense. They are the reservoirs of individuality, the springs of difference
on which freedom and creative imagination de-
pend. Those, let it be remembered, do not come
into play through the uninterrupted flow of a
single tradition and habit of life. Where that

is isolated, uninterrupted, unchallenged, no thought is born, nothing of high order, as the critics of American civilization complain of America, is created. Freedom and creative imagination crown only the confrontation of traditions and habits of life; the assimilation of one culture but not of one people, into the body and soul of another. New England went to Europe, the Middle West to New England, Europe, a low and peasant Europe perhaps, but the subsoil which aristocratic Europe grew and fed on, to the Middle West. If what comes of this clash and compenetration is not so very high, it is none the less a growth of the soil, a portent and promise of the country's future.

The races of Europe have now for a generation been grouped upon the American continent, among Americans, in patterns not so unlike those they brought from home. The generation is at its first flowering in things of the spirit, in works of art and of science. Can it be that the freshness, the candor, the poignancy and beauty as well as the strangeness of this flowering have no relation to the contrasted doctrines and disciplines of the communities living in the land, nourishing one another's spirits through mutual contagion? Surely, the more cohesive and flexible, the more adjustable and self-sustaining are these communities, the more certain it is that the

men and women they intimately breed shall bring
a richer, a more sustained and masterlike endowment into the wider ranges of the national
life and the national letters. The Jewish community, the most cohesive and the most adapta-
ble of the non-British communities in America,
is said not only to have contributed largely to
the fine arts of the nation, but to have in its own
existence been already stimulated to new forms
of life and growth. "In our examination of the
Jewish type of organization," Messrs. Parks and
Miller declare, "we gain an impression that the
experiments of this community upon its own
problems contain an interest not limited to the
Jewish community, but extending to American
society as a whole. . . . In the case of the Jewish groups we find spontaneous, intelligent and
highly organized experiments in democratic control which may assume the character of a permanent contribution to the organization of the
American State."

If then cultural history and the American
present are any index, the cultural prospect has
been enriched, not depleted by the immigration,
settlement, and self-maintenance in communities
of the peoples of all Europe upon the North
American continent. The pioneer Puritan and
the puritan Pioneer have thereby received their
foils. Color and import have been added to life

in the United States, and if the spirit of a co-
operative liberty can be poured into the folkways
of the British stock and insured in continuance
among the others, the national fellowship of cultural diversities should eventually come to fulfillment in a truly "trans-national America," a new
and happy form of associative harmony. But—
can such a spirit be poured into such bottles, and
can such bottles hold such a spirit?

IV

THE NEWEST REACTION[1]

I

IF thirty American intellectuals are to be believed, their country is in a bad way indeed. The picture they draw of civilization in the United States is sad and drab and snappy. Its blacks are so very, very black, and its whites so dirty gray. In fact, the few hopeful things they mention are mostly by way of being programs of reform. Some virtue is found in victrolas, player-pianos and motion-picture orchestras, in the metropolitan theater and in advertising, and much is made of the "contempt of the younger people for their elders." Otherwise, there is nothing, it would seem, except Puritanism, materialism, vulgarity and wealth in which the United States excels. Even the last of these virtues is not unmitigated, for the country presents to-day the spectacle of a land ruined by over-plenty, the farmers of Kansas and Iowa

---

[1] *Civilization in the United States. An Inquiry by Thirty Americans.* Edited by Harold Stearns. New York: Harcourt, Brace and Co.

burning corn for fuel while the workers of New York and Pennsylvania are suffering for lack of food. The reason is that the national economy is under the rule of financiers who control the flow of credit and so the destinies of agriculture and industry. As they are concerned solely about profits, they make advantages for the investor and waste for the worker. Affairs go through periodic cycles of alternate expansion and contraction, activity and speculation being succeeded by unemployment and failure. Here and there government is called in to interfere in business. But to what avail? The business cycle is a vicious circle of which the agencies designed to break it become themselves a part. Besides, there is no hope of government, for, owing to the localism of the Constitution, we are ruled by "cheap, common, ignorant, scoundrelly Congressmen" who, among other horrors and injustices could perpetrate such a thing as the eighteenth amendment! Then again, our thrift is undermined and our evil nature solicited by "America's cruelest and most ruthless sport, religion or profession," advertising. This, "with an accurate stroke but with a perverted intent, . . . coddles and toys with all that is base and gross in our physical and spiritual compositions." By means of it business dominates our press, and our press, our most persistent continuous influence, is rendered thereby untrustworthy, cowardly and dishonest. Business makes of our cities ugly industrial aggregations in which the hotel and theater districts are the "real civic centers," and of our small towns poor imitations of the cities or leaves them as mere social units delighting in conventions, parades, picnics and old home weeks.

The people who inhabit these towns and cities are a heterogeneous multitude whose prevalent modes of association are those of the Elk, the Moose, the Mason and the other totemic fraternities. They compose families growing constantly smaller in size and briefer in duration. Marriage is late and factories and offices more and more compete with homes for the employment of wives. Nevertheless, the whole country suffers from "nerves" because it is given over to "too much mother-love," to say nothing of the strain and compulsion that arise from the maladjustment to each other of the diverse racial and economic groups, particularly the immigrants and the aristocrats. In addition, there is no clear recognition in American morality of the true implications of sex. This morality imposes either repression or deception, and with repression comes perversion and with perversion an intensified susceptibility to mob-mindedness. The freedom of association among the young, again, which means courtship without consummation, necessitates a balancing by consummation without courtship. Hence the institutions of sex life compel woman always to be either prostitute or wife, in effect sequestering her and thus keeping her from growing up. Sex life in the United States is in a state of arrested development.

If it isn't so for the immigrant when he arrives here, it becomes so, it may be inferred, when he has lived here. But the immigrant is hurt in other ways. He migrates to escape the oppression of the landlord at home only to come under the oppression of the industrialist abroad. He performs the hard and "dirty" work of the country in mine and mill under impossible conditions. When he seeks to improve these conditions he is hounded and denounced. The phrase "likely to become a public charge" is held over his head and is used to compel his acquiescence in a condition no better than peonage, without right even to an opinion unacceptable to authority. When finally he does become domiciled in the country, he is fortunate if he does not belong to a conspicuous racial minority like the Oriental, the negro, or the Jew. If he does, and he shows any signs of power or competency in competition with the racial majority, he becomes subject to invidious distinctions, a victim of race prejudice. The South, fearing the potential power of the negro, disfranchises him and keeps him in practical slavery. The whole country, feeling the successful competition of the Jew, becomes anti-Semitic. And so it goes. Remedies only serve to intensify the disease, sæcula sæculorum, world without end.

For the law is helpless to correct an evil like this, and education is in worse case than law. The life of the pioneer, the psychology of the immigrant, the interest of big business, all serve to invest the United States with the temper of lawlessness. This lawlessness is enhanced by the fact that American law is antiquated and thus irrelevant to American life. As for education— it is the dominant superstition of our time. Its authority has been set in human reason as salvation from social sin, but in fact it is sold unto the devil of the vested interests of mind and pocket. It aims not at truth, but at conformity. In the grade schools it is a regimentation of the mind; in the institutions of the higher learning it is directly a servant of the interests. As a national institution it is "the propaganda department of the state and the existing social system," imposing over-specialization on the pupils and indignity on the teachers.

II

Under such circumstances, what can one expect of scholarship and criticism, of science, of
philosophy, of engineering, of medicine, of arts
and letters? Nothing better than the worst.
"America has a body and no soul," therefore
many professors and no scholars. Its criticism suffers from "a want of philosophic insight
and precision," a need of education in "esthetic
thinking," even as its scholarship requires deeper
sensibility and taste. Its science, while industri-
ous, and significant in experimental biology,
psychology and anthropology, is a mere epiphe-
nomenon, not an organic product of the soil. It
lacks an encouraging public with a basic theo-
retical training. It lacks leisure, freedom,
breadth, self-criticism, and "reasoned non-con-
formism." History, again, having been con-
taminated from Germany, has become dull and
is devoted to the service of the vested interests.
So is engineering, because the engineers are em-
ployees merely, servile in mind, politically uneducated, and without the power of self-criticism.
And as for medicine—of all professions, the doctors are lowest in intelligence. Exercising a
quasi-religious function, they are given over to
medical fads and manias, devoted to "ga-ga-
isms," and they are restrained by moralistic

biases from honest and effective work in preventive medicine. At the same time our writers are incapacitated from leading the literary life because they become slaves "to some demand from without," so that the creative spirit in them is rendered impotent at its very beginnings. Moved by fear rather than by faith, they have no power of growth. The pioneer past and the business present abort the "creative career." Writers are too weak to withstand their drain and solicitation. The "intellectual life" is too auxiliary to business. Thus philosophy itself, in its most representative phase, i. e., its more than professorial phase, is preoccupied with results, and its head is diminished by the lack of a metaphysics. Economic opinion, while showing signs of awakening to economic facts and their implications, is prevailingly "the case for capitalism" or the case against it. And the case against it, as "radicalism," is irrelevant and immaterial because of the mental traits of its proponents in theory and practice, because of their "remoteness from reality." The residue—"the things of the mind and the spirit," "the intellectual life" *an und für sich* which preoccupies Mr. Stearns—this has been "given over . . . into the almost exclusive control of women." Americans have nothing else to do but make money; their women nothing else but to spend it. They spend it on

hunting culture.   From them issues the tone of
American art, philosophy, music, education, of
everything "intellectual."   Men who concern
themselves with such things therefore become ef-
feminate and the things themselves are perverted
from noble uselessness to ignoble application.
For women demand service from everything,
even from "introspection, contemplation, or
scrupulous adherence to logical sequence," which
ought to be like the lilies of the field.   Such are
the dire effects of the pioneer past and the business present!   America suffers from a "balked
disposition to think."

There's music, for instance.   Music costs the
United States more than it costs any other country on earth.   The composer gets every encouragement.   Does he therefore produce?   Not a bit.
He lacks training and discipline; his taste is
vicious and his workmanship is bad; he has no intellectual competency.   An illiterate public, composed mostly of women, deprave and inhibit him,
for they require their music to serve as an escape
from pioneer and puritan settings.   The professional inadequacy of the music critics and the
music journals inhibits him.   And particularly is
he inhibited by the racial heterogeneity of the
American people.   For the creation of music requires a background of common "esthetic emotion" and such common emotion is possible only

to a common stock uttering itself in a common musical idiom—not negro or Indian or foreign —but American. Thus music is in a parlous case. But then, there's art. Art is painting and painters here have no foundation and no tradition, are subject to the vicious influence of a female public and undergo scornful tolerance at the hands of males for, one supposes, the women's sake. And the theater! What good there's in it is largely due to the metropolis and the foreigners. Its great bad is the consequence of the depraved tastes of the provinces, with their lascivious puritanism and hypocrisy; of the greed of the playwrights who, eager for money-successes, turn out bad workmanship and no ideas; of the disregard of the newspapers that treat the theaters shabbily as to space and cut their reviews to the measure of the business-office returns. Or take sport and play. How can a people with so little imagination in their heads and so much hero-worship in their hearts prefer playing themselves to paying others to play for them? And as for humor—it is to laugh. How can a thing like that, "a thing of all times and all places," be degraded to local quality and flavor? There is Attic salt in Mark Twain and, one infers, American pep in Aristophanes.

Poetry alone would seem to be relatively untainted by the fatal inadequacy or deformity which besets the above-mentioned elements of American civilization. The American scene, we are told, is not a unity but a multiplicity, each part self-sustaining and self-expressive, each possessed of its own tone and tempo. American poetry utters the diversity of the American scene. It is an art without tradition, springing directly from the soil, but influenced and fertilized from Europe. Its qualities are health, energy, vigor, vitality, self-confidence and copiousness. Beginning as a reaction against the prettiness of the verse of 1890-1910, it for a while made a fetish of the ugly and a cult of rebellion. Then, as it began to find itself for itself, it turned, in the work of Robinson, Frost and Masters, to the dramatic apprehension of reality; in that of Fletcher, Pound, Bodenheim, H. D., Amy Lowell, to the presentation of color; in that of Eliot, Kreymborg and Stevens to the expression of subtle psychologizings; in that of Carl Sandburg, to social responsibility; in that of Vachel Lindsay to "rhythmic abandon mixed with evangelism." The "anarchy of the poetic community" is, it will be seen, great, but its achievement is "healthy." It could profit by a developed sense of workmanship and a diminished preoccupation with matters not intrinsic to its task. Particularly would it benefit by "a fusion of the extraordinary range of poetic virtues with which

our contemporary poets confront us, into one
poetic consciousness." Poetry needs, in a word,
a single ethos, but whether our many cultures can
or should give rise to a single ethos is an open
question.

III

Readers who are depressed by this sketch from
the portrait of our United States by thirty
American intellectuals may find relief by turning to the portrait itself. For I have been at
pains to give the sketch some logical sequence,
some structure which the portrait itself does not
possess and which may well belie its essential
nature and intent. I have made it far more like
a composite photograph than it really is, and the
parts far more interpenetrative and interdependent, a thing not to be done without much possible
injustice to the writers, who are of very varied
ages and far more varied endowments. Among
them are figures as contrasted as Harold Stearns
and Harold Brown, H. L. Mencken and Katha-
rine Anthony, Ring Lardner and Robert Lowie,
Anonymous and J. E. Spingarn. One wonders
what the devil some of them, like Walton Hamilton or Zechariah Chafee or Conrad Aiken or
Robert Lovett or Garet Garrett or Geroid
Robinson—to mention the most outstanding—
are doing in that gallery, so seasoned and in-

formed do their essays appear; so considered, by contrast, their judgments.

If the dissertations of which this volume consists are a basis of judgment, the unity of the writers is not consensus deriving from a common understanding and philosophy of life and a common love of excellence. It appears rather as a common and usually justifiable discontent voiced with a more or less common sharpness, a discontent directed at the very apparent evil on the surfaces and last terms of things American rather than at their fundamentals, unless loading "pioneer conditions" and "business" with the burden of national sin may be called a regard for fundamentals. Such a loading is too traditional, too obvious and facile, and too right for other places as well, to be particularly significant. And beyond this—the text does not make it appear that its authors have worked out any fundamentals. Neither in the topics treated nor in the order of their succession does any principle seem to have been employed or any vision followed. Indeed, the arrangement of the book is even more haphazard and idiosyncratic than the categories of its subject-matter. Perhaps the authors drews lots for place, or its editor was left to exercise his unmitigated taste and judgment; certainly no other principle of order, whether logical or alphabetical, seems to have been followed. The omissions, moreover, are very conspicuous—some, much more conspicuous than the inclusions. Mr. Stearns is conscious of the omission of religion; he excuses it by explaining that nobody that he invited would undertake to deal with it. But neither he nor his associates seem to be at all aware of the significance of the failure to treat, in a study of the civilization of the United States, the nature and implications of institutions so fundamental and characteristic as its agricultural economy and its labor movement, to say nothing of its architecture, its motion-picture industry, and its secondary arts. To pass these by in a work like this with an allusion here and there and by the way, or with a sneer, is to convict oneself at once of superficiality and irrelevance.

If, then, I have given the summary of this indictment of civilization in the United States a unity which the indictment itself does not possess, I have done so at the risk of some injustice, inevitable, yet, I think, sufficiently authorized. For Mr. Harold Stearns, in his introduction, describes the book as an "adventure in intellectual coöperation." He tells of frequent meetings in his home, and of discovering "even at our first meeting . . . our points of view to have so much in common." He speaks of his own supervisory labors in behalf of unity and declares that, in

view of the high individualism and freedom of
opinion of each writer, "the underlying unity
which binds the volume together is really sur-
prising." This unity he expresses in the following propositions. First: that there is a
dichotomy between preaching and practice in the
United States. Second: that American civilization is not Anglo-Saxon. Third: that the
American population suffers from emotional and
esthetic starvation. How he distilled these
propositions from the contents of the book is a
mystery I cannot penetrate; how by means of
them he could distinguish American civilization
from British or continental I cannot discover.
However, there they are, vocal of the unity of
thirty intellectuals. The hypothesis of its existence is further enforced by a significant reference. Mr. Stearns declares himself and his
fellow-adventurers to have been animated by the
spirit and temper of the French Encyclopedists;
and the publisher's puff describes the book as a
"revaluation of our contemporary culture" in
that spirit.

The description, of course, enlivens our hopes
and invites our mind. It conspicuously challenges a comparison. But alas, how you are mis-
led! Here is no philosophic synthesis of new life
and new knowledge used to judge ancient privilege and antiquated institutions. Here is no

sage and witty scholarship, no reasoned irony
and satirical tolerance compact at once of sympathy and judgment, which are the attributes of
the Encyclopedists. You find yourself, on the
contrary, compelled to the inference that all that
most of our adventurers ever saw of the Encyclopedists was the name in a book. Their disesteem
of civilization in the United States contains so
many things that the Encyclopedists were at
pains to condemn that they appear in the cool dry
light of the eighteenth-century enlightenment as
a sort of Pococurantist club, a mob-Pococurante
—with a difference.

Pococurante is a figure in Voltaire's *Candide,*
that stingingly urbane arraignment of eighteenth-
century civilization which nevertheless concluded
that the whole lesson of life is the principle that
it is necessary to cultivate one's own garden.
One day Candide and his friend Martin pay
Pococurante a visit. They find a personage who
can see little virtue in women, painting, music,
philosophy, poetry, science or literature of his
own or any other time. As the visit ends Candide
whispers to Martin: "Oh, what a superior person!
What a great genius to be sure is this Pococurante! Nothing can please him!" A moment
later he adds, "There, you will agree with me, is
the happiest man in the world, and he is looking
down upon all his possessions." To which Martin

replies: "Do you not see that he is disgusted with
everything he has? Plato remarked long ago that
it is not the healthiest stomach which rejects all
food." "But," Candide returns, "is there no
pleasure in criticizing everything, in perceiving
faults where all other men think there are beau-
ties?" "Which is as much as to say," retorts
Martin, "that there must be some pleasure in
never being pleased."

IV

This citation from the greatest of the Encyclopedists might well be the last word on the American book indited in their spirit were it not that
the spirit of this book is that spirit with such a
difference. It is the difference that elicits further consideration. For the difference is that the
book is not, like the work of the Encyclopedists, simply a diagnosis, but a symptom as well.
The work of the Encyclopedists was a true diagnosis. It entailed and expressed positive standards of social and intellectual health by which it
measured disease. There was no mistaking or
evading these standards. Our adventurers, on
the contrary, set forth nothing positive, nothing
of articulate excellence. They condemn; they
denounce; they excommunicate. But their action is a passion, not a judgment, the work of re-

bellion and disaffection which must reject and
tear down rather than build upon what exists,
which has no eye for the other, equally real, aspects of what they doom, in which, so often, are
the promise and even the growth of appropriate
future excellence. If they cherish positive ideals
at all, those can be discerned only from what
they repudiate. They make use, it is true, of
such terms as "culture," "the intellectual life,"
"the creative life," "the good life," but they leave
you to discover what they mean by them only by
negative implication and allusion in transit.
These drive you, if you want a positive content
for those terms, to look for it, not in Europe
(for Europe is in fact, though our adventurers
do not, in the glamor of distance, seem to know
it, no less under the domination of business than
the United States), but in China perhaps, or in
India, or if you must have Europe, in the Europe of pre-industrial times. But the intellectuals and esthetes of China and India and pre-
industrial Europe were also not without their
plaints, if their poets and philosophers may be
trusted. Instead of the business men there were
the mandarin and the lord of the manor, also de-
grading "culture" and keeping artist or thinker
as a servant in the house and a decoration in the
state, restricting his freedom and perverting his
creative genius. "People of quality," says the

would-be teacher of Jeannot to his parents, upon whom he is urging that Jeannot need be taught only the art of making himself agreeable, "people of quality, if they are rich enough, know everything without learning anything because, in point of fact and in the long run, they are masters of all knowledge which they can command and pay for."

Since Voltaire made this observation, artists and thinkers, like other craftsmen, have been cut loose from the service and patronage of people of quality. Their dependence has become indirect and more flexible. They are more definitely on their own, and their livelihoods are contingent on a wider and more diversified public. In the common economy of a democratized, complicated industrial world they rank as craftsmen struggling for a market for the products of head and hand. Their task is more than ever communication, not soliloquy, communication to a public of highly variable range in depth of thought and sensibility, with an average of refinement and spirit inevitably lower than those of the classes of other civilizations and with individual differences of greater scope and subtlety. For the heightening and liberation of individuality and the expansion of mediocrity are concomitant phenomena. All sorts of things get produced and get hearings which would have been unthink-

able in the age of homogeneous leisure classes
and illiterate masses. The esthetic mortality is
correspondingly higher, also. Of the infinite deal
that is brought forth much less survives, the
turn-over is so rapid, the struggle for differen-
tiation and place so poignant. And all the while,
under the stress of the industrial reorganization
of society, "culture," "the intellectual life," the
"creative life," are diverging into a different content and direction, are acquiring, therefore, a
different meaning.

Those who are attuned to this new thing utter it in forms compensatory or expressive; in
them—the poets, for example—is the promise
of the excellence that always supervenes as the
maturity of whatever is dynamic in the institutions of human life. Those who are not attuned,
whether through temperament or training or
habit, are thrown out of gear by it, and spend
themselves in motion without movement, like a
motor-car with its wheels in the air. They become filled with uneasiness and resentment and
unable to discover any virtue or promise in what
so obfuscates them. They have no idea that it
is to be mastered. They think only that it is to
be evaded or destroyed. They hark back to a
past where it did not exist, therefore to them, a
happier past. Thus it is significant that of our
thirty adventurers the best-tempered and the

most judicial appear to be the youngest, who grew up when the industrial *milieu* was already established, or the oldest, whom it came too late essentially to affect; they see ways for improvement and propose reforms. It is the men on the edge of middle age or over it who seem to be the shrillest and most violent in their disaffection and harp most regretfully upon the forgotten valuations of their youth. These are they who in school and college and afield would have suffered most from the dislocation caused by industry and resent most its attrition of their endowment and sidetracking of their training. The latter, willy-nilly, supplied them with their standards, and though these may seem forgotten they operate and make culture and the intellectual life mean to them the genteel occupations and avocations of the pre-industrial aristocracies, vanished from New England, but whose not uncontaminated survival in Europe sheds for them a glamor upon the European scene. The father of their illusion was Aristotle, the traditional lawgiver to the cultural life of Europe, who, teacher and companion of aristocrats himself, assumed that thought could not be free unless it was useless, or culture real unless it was irresponsible. His predecessor, Socrates, knew better, for he taught that that is not good which is good for nothing. He felt and understood and

expressed the dynamic relevance to one another of individual and community and the interchangeable and interpenetrative behavior of
means and ends. He set no ends outside the individual and conceived no individuality that was
not coöperatively social. It was in this that he,
and Plato when Plato was most definitely under
the Socratic influence, envisaged the good life.
So the Encyclopedists understood "the good
life" too. But critics like Mr. Stearns and Mr.
Mencken and Mr. Van Wyck Brooks, to mention those of our adventurers whose measures of
value are most definite and public, seem not to
have profited by their example. They seem to
fancy that the "intellectual life" or "the creative
life" is a content rather than an activity and that
that is no culture or bad culture which does not
express the age of the landed gentry and illiterate
peasants rather than the age of the moneyed
bourgeois and lettered proletarians. They seem
to imagine, when they are constructive, that individuality is an absolutely independent variable
and that a *milieu* can offer an artist nothing positive which he cannot draw from his inner consciousness. They know better, and on occasion
they think and say better. But their feelings
are too much engaged. Disaffected, lacking
poise of intellect and serenity of spirit, they
figure in this book, in effect, as emotional reac-

tionaries. They look backward, not forward.
Their reaction has novelty because they desire
to sustain bygone ideals by rejecting the *status
quo* rather than by conserving it. Their attitude
is a paradox which would never have arisen had
their spirit and temper been more like that of
Encyclopedists and less like that of romantic
amateurs, crying their woes. Then they would,
like the Encyclopedists (they were so called because they wrote an encyclopedia), have in-
formed themselves, and have worked into a
philosophy commonly held, of whatever is to-
day known about the mind and body of man, his
institutions, his endeavor and the conditions of
his endeavor's success, and in the explicit light of
this philosophy spoken judgment on civilization
in the United States. Instead, their rebellious
passion has led them to disregard all that is
dynamic in their land, all that the future promises fruition in, for the sake of outcry of their
woe. Perhaps this is as it should be. For strong
emotion is purged by utterance, and it would be
no more than fair to regard this plaint of the disaffected as, on the whole, nothing more than a
purge. Now that they have come clean—if they
have come clean—perhaps they will consult William James's *On a Certain Blindness in Human
Beings* and try again.

V

AMERICA AND THE LIFE OF
REASON [1]

I

FROM his dark and revolutionary beginnings
the American has been a puzzle to himself and
to his neighbors. It was not the new world of
his habitation which caused the puzzlement, nor
the old world of his heritage. The former was
as the earth is everywhere; the steppes of Russia
and the midcontinental plains of North America
set men the same task and they performed it with
their bare hands in about the same way. The latter he carried with him in his heart, and he uttered his heart in his life for a long time, quite as
the European did, generosity for generosity
and brutality for brutality, combining loving
thoughts with hateful actions, noble professions
with mean conduct, law with violence, religion
with cruelty, morality with dishonesty, after the
manner of men everywhere. The Colonial of the
United States was merely a European in an un-
European setting. He built himself his foreign

[1] Reprinted from the *Journal of Philosophy*, Vol. XVIII, Nos.
20, 21.

quarter as Europeans do in China to-day, and save that the land he built it in was empty of men instead of peopled, he behaved in the same way. The Puritans prayed and persecuted, the Cavaliers drank and dallied, the Scotch-Irish renewed their Ulster, with Indians instead of Southrors to battle against and hunt.

Europe gave no thought to the otherness of America until there had been added to the life there established and the purposes gained a new idea and a new hope, and this hope and idea had been ordained by choice and consent the mark of distinction, the differentia of the species, wherewith white men in America set themselves apart from their blood brothers in Europe. The hope and idea are constituted by what is usually called democracy.

When the Americans elected to give it allegiance and to order—or confuse—their lives by its dogmas and practices it was a new thing in Europe, the challenge of present thought to old institutions, nowhere tested in action or established in conduct. The American Revolution was an adventure into the political unknown, as the Russian Revolution is to-day, and its fortunes became a matter of momentous import both to the privileged who were secure in the old order and to the disinherited who hoped for security in a new. It could not be assaulted by its neighbors as were the French Revolution and the Russian; it was too far, and the distances of its domicile were too vast. It could only be watched, and praised or execrated. And because it was thus isolate and unique in an elsewhere crowded and jostling world, it became what later polities, peopled by the same original stocks and undertaking much the same adventure, what Canada and Australia and South Africa and New Zealand did not become, a symbol and a portent of a new turn in the organization of western society, whose fortunes must decide whether life and liberty and the pursuit of happiness are inalienable rights or lucky accidents, whether government should be a device which makes and keeps them secure for all men or takes them away from many men so that they may be assured to some; whether its powers rest on the consent of the governed or the will and cunning of the governors. Having hitched its wagon to the glittering, imaginative luminaries of the Declaration of Independence, the American republic, its institutions, its life and fortune, have undergone scrutiny of a type unparalleled by other states. It has become a puzzle, whose duplexity and contradictions one writer after another has tried to extend or to reconcile—De Tocqueville and Bryce, Dickens and Kipling and Wells, to speak of only the most notable of the aliens; Irving and

Lowell and Whitman, Howells and Mark Twain, to speak only of the generations gone, in America.

To the list of the most distinguished, domestic and stranger, must now be added Mr. George Santayana,[1] taking his place between them. I say "between" because Mr. Santayana does not feel himself to be an American. "I am not one," he writes, "except by long association." Yet it is apparent that this long association has much affected his own temperament and opinions, blinding him to some things and making him more sensitive to others, in such a way that, if during his forty years in the United States he did not become an American, he certainly ceased to be a European. Perhaps he never was a European of the contemporary mode. Both his method and his manner point to a quality of personality unassimilable to the categorical groupings of the present time, with its passion, its strain, its speed, its hard venturesomeness, its reticulated, yet abandoned realism. Those who remember him in the class-room will remember him as a spirit solemn, and sweet and withdrawn; whose Johannine face by a Renaissance painter held an abstracted eye and a hieratic smile, half mischief, half content; whose rich voice flowed

[1] George Santayana: *Character and Opinion in the United States.* New York: Charles Scribner's Sons, 1920.

evenly, in cadences smooth and balanced as a
liturgy; whose periods had the intricate perfection of a poem and the import of a prophecy;
who spoke somehow for his hearers and not to
them, stirring the depths of their natures and
troubling their minds, as an oracle might, to
whom pertained mystery and reverence, so compact of remoteness and fascination did he seem, so
moving, and so unmoved. Between him and them
there was a bar for which I know no similitude
save that which is suggested sometimes by a
Chinese painting of the tranquil Enlightened
One, the irresistible magnet of his sedulous devotees, filling their vision and drawing them on
as he sits, inscrutably smiling, above them. This
detachment, which often seemed to me to have a
tinge of sadness and insufficiency in it, is a quality of all of Mr. Santayana's works and endows
them with something of the passionate impersonality of great music.

At the points where it is personal it is felt as
a provocative superiority or a somewhat pitying,
somewhat ironical comprehension, like that of a
knowing spectator at the play. It suggests a
kinship there, in which learning and experience
both are mingled. You are led to think of the
age of Voltaire, and of Voltaire himself, of Voltaire withdrawn from indignation and with a
malice more Olympian. And you are led to

think of the age of Emerson, and of Emerson himself, but of an Emerson turned luminous and balanced and articulate, with an understanding more precise and a sympathy more skeptical. In both these periods, the period of Voltaire and the period of Emerson, men of sensibility and insight found themselves in a society whose institutions were surviving without being alive, whose visions had hardened into formulæ and whose powers had become privileges. In both, feeling was turning to rebellion and hope to protest. The men of sensibility and insight were those who could find place in neither camp of the dividing society. They stood aside from both authority and rebellion. They converted feeling into understanding and hope into philosophic irony. The perspectives they found turned authority to ridicule and rebellion to pity.

This also is what Mr. Santayana, at his most humane, accomplishes, and far more perfectly than his predecessors. He carries over into the twentieth century, as a pitying detachment of free intelligence from rebellion, the detachment which free intelligence in nineteenth-century New England accomplished from authority. So he stands alone, without party, sect or school, a humanist against all narrower allegiances, and as lonely in his being as his vision is great. Neither James nor Royce, who were his colleagues as well

as his teachers at Harvard, has this loneliness.
The former was a rebel and founded a school; the
latter was an authoritarian and perpetuated one.
Emerson does have this loneliness; he moved beyond the range of established authority by being
different, not by being opposed, and it is in the
line of Emerson that the spiritual genealogy of
Santayana, the American, is to be sought. Of
course, there are contributing branches: race, the
discipline and forgotten impressions of childhood,
the isolation and otherness of the youthful newcomer in a strange community, the richness and
refinement of a learning and a culture without
parallel among philosophers anywhere, and a
pondering of the insight and the glories of Plato
and Aristotle, the Greeks, and the austerities
and insight of Spinoza the Jew. But the essential assurance of the goodness of life, the recognition of its youth, its spontaneity and its abso-
luteness, the readiness to excuse, to condone, and
to adjust, to seek composition and harmony as
against conflict and intransigency, these are of
the same spirit as that which Mr. Santayana attributes to America, particularly the America
which he knew and grew up in. It is the spirit
of Emerson, unstained by the oversoul.

Its philosophical garb and expression, which
give it so subtle and fascinating a manner and
accent, point, while they blur, the figure and senti-

ment they adorn—and conceal. For in his confrontation with life, Mr. Santayana has himself not escaped the contagion of the genteel tradition. The Jehovah of Calvin has been displaced by the matter of Aristotle and Spinoza and modern science, the predestination of Presbyterianism by the necessities of automatism. Mankind, for him, is what it is, and will be what it must. Its history has only an expressive, not an operative significance; its moral best is beauty rather than goodness; consummation, not achievement. "Every animal has his festive and ceremonious moments, when he poses or plumes himself or thinks; sometimes he even sings and flies aloft in a sort of ecstasy. Somewhat in the same way, when reflection in man becomes dominant, it may become passionate; it may become religion or philosophy—adventures often more thrilling than the humdrum experiences they are supposed to interrupt."

For Mr. Santayana conceives life as the heirs of the genteel tradition among whom he lived and with whom he grew up lived it; vertically, not horizontally. "Reflection," he says, "is itself a turn, and the top turn, given to life." He means that we grow into thought as a lily grows into blossom. Its roots reach out into the mud, its stalk stretches upward through slime; but its petals are in the free air, all white and

pure and well-ordered. In them the matter or
force underneath has come to the limit of its
power, has used itself up. They neither toil nor
spin, they simply are, the topmost turn given to
life. So also is reflection in man the passionate
but important excellence of a living body whose
energies have somewhat exceeded its needs and
blossomed in spirit—the topmost turn given to
life—as the height and shape and iridescence and
music of a fountain are the topmost turn of the
water-pressure whose ultimate expression these
are. It is of the essence of reason to live on this
topmost turn. It is to make of life a harmony
and to find habitation in the ideal, and this is
what the heirs of the genteel tradition and its
victims had somehow come to when Mr. Santayana knew them and dwelt among them. That
he should have escaped their contagion would
have argued an insensitiveness altogether contrary to his nature: his very strictures upon them
show how deeply they influenced him. What he
says of Charles Eliot Norton, who was one of
the New England apostles of the "top turn,"
may be said, I think, also of him: "Professor
Norton's mind was deeply moralized, discriminating and sad; and these qualities rightly
seemed American to the French observer of New
England, but they rightly seemed un-American
to the politician from Washington." It may be

said, with, of course, a difference, but it is not, to my mind, a difference of the kind or degree to make of Mr. Santayana a species of another genus or to insulate him from the tradition that pervaded the scene in which he grew up.

II

The duplexity of American life of which Charles Eliot Norton is a concretion and a symbol has its mates in other fields. Of the divinities in the Pantheon which the myth-making public-school histories of the United States have provided for its public men, who could be more diverse and dissonant in temperament and aspiration than Washington, Lincoln and Roosevelt; and which of them is the "true" American? Lincoln, deeply moralized, discriminating and sad, whom also politicians acknowledge as the foremost personification of the type, yet whose life and labor entail everything that is the opposite of Norton's? Roosevelt, the nervous and didactic confutation of Lincoln's tolerance, sadness and quiet? Or Washington, with the broad solidity, the heavy thoroughness of an English squire, in all respects the reverse of Roosevelt's swiftness, shrillness, instability and omnivorous superficiality? Or, to take a later instance— Wilson, with the professions and ideology he

took to the Peace Conference and the engage-
ments he brought back from there? Or a sym-
bolic one—the statue made by the sculptor Bar-
tholdi as the gift of the free Republic of France
to the sister-republic across the sea—Liberty,
enlightening the world, with a detention camp at
its base?

The interpretation of this duplexity which Mr.
Santayana offers is the traditional one. Character and opinion in America are, in his regard,
the outcome of the impact of an old, rather
overcivilized people upon a new and undeveloped
land. The force of the impact loosened, the attrition of the contact frayed, the ancestral hope,
habit and custom of life and thought, generating
others, more competent for the necessities of the
setting, truer to the coercions and more answera-
ble to the requirements of its nature. The generation of these others was a renovation of the
youth of the people. Americans are a sort of
collective Faust, whose memories of Gretchen
and the cloister trouble but do not restrain the
conquest of the new empire and, perhaps, the
endeavor after Helen. America is a young
country with old memories. The duplexity is
due to the conflict between this—somewhat magical—joining of crude youthful passions and polite, ancient thoughts and shibboleths in one
body-politic. The classes who utter the pas-

sions and those who utter the memories are not at one, and the future, of course, belongs to youth.

I am not sure that in restating Mr. Santayana's allusive and varied formulations of this view I have done him justice. His thought is too organic, too integrated with provisos and qualifications to be susceptible of simple, inevitable statement. The essential point seems to me, however, beyond doubt. It is this confrontation of new land and old people, and most of his discussion consists of the delineation and, in the light of the harmonies of the life of reason, which is his measure of all things human and divine, of the interpretation, of the changes in the people brought about by the contact with the land.

How profound these changes are, what they signify, how lasting they are likely to be, is not clear. Sometimes he suggests that they are altogether external, and that the inwardness of human existence is a thing inalterably young: "Nothing lasts forever; but the elasticity of life is wonderful, and even if the world lose its memory, it could not lose its youth"; so that America is exemplifying anew an immemorial cycle of destruction and restoration that life forever undergoes. At other times there is a hint that the changes he speaks of are constitutive, and that the species *homo Americanus* is compact really of these and nothing else, so that persons of whatever stock suffer a sea-change and indifferently become American: "Young America was originally composed of all the prodigals, truants, and adventurous spirits that the colonial families produced: it was fed continually by the younger generation, born in a spacious, half-empty world, tending to forget the old, straitened morality and to replace it by another, quite jovially human. This truly native America was reënforced by the miscellany of Europe arriving later, not in the hope of founding a godly commonwealth, but only of prospering in an untrammeled one. The horde of immigrants accepts the external arrangements and social spirit of American life, but it never hears of its original austere principles, or it relegates them to the same willing oblivion as it does the constraints which it has just escaped—Jewish, Irish, German, Italian, or whatever else they be."

But, internal or external, these changes are not, we are asked to believe, so discontinuous as this passage implies. The English stock which first settled the country brought with it and preserved unchanged and caused to prosper, the spirit of "English liberty." It is by virtue of this spirit and its supremacy in America that the miscellany of Europe could become the solidarity of the United States, Americans all, regard-

less of origin or trend. Its manifestation is free
coöperation, based on free individuality. It requires plasticity and a willingness to consult, to
compromise, to decide by majority vote. It cannot prevail where minorities are unable loyally to
acquiesce in the decision of the majority. And
in practice its essence is this acquiescence.
Where it does not prevail, the liberty desired or
hoped for is "absolute or revolutionary liberty,"
which is unyielding, intransigent, violent and
selfish, capable of inspired vision and relentless
martyrdom, but not of organized, harmonious
living. Absolute liberty is a goal; English liberty is a method or technique which men may
use in adapting themselves to one another and
to the world at large. It is blind, illogical, piece-
meal, for its principle is simply that of "live and
let live." The organization it effects presents
like the British Empire the motley pattern of a
crazy-quilt; the institutions it generates are
clumsy, "jumbled and limping." It always
leaves a residue, unsocialized and unordered.
Resting on respect for individuality, the contacts
it involves are external and there remains room
in it for growth. Its sign here in America is the
triviality or technicality of legislative measures,
the fact that government has so long "been carried on in the shade, by persons of no name or
dignity." For "free government works well in

proportion as it is superfluous," and the notorious superfluity of government in the United States is a sign "that coöperative liberty is working well and rendering overt government unnecessary."

Is it, however, such a sign? The observation goes deep to signalize how American is Mr. Santayana's opinion about America. For America is not yet, and never so far has been, the crowded country that England always was, where different stocks of ancient root have been pressed one against the other to live together as best they might—together, and yet free. America has been an empty land, where diverse liberties could coöperate because they had ample space and did not need to touch or crowd. Nor because, for the most part, government in the United States was so long weak and far-removed, was its rigor absent. The rigor came, however, not through its officers, by due process of law, but through law's violators, at the hands of Judge Lynch. And that symbol of the spirit of coöperative liberty is still prominently with us, as it was in the beginning, and seems like to be in days to come, one hundred per cent American. Nor does Judge Lynch live alone, nor is he without children in the house, from the Ku Klux to the industrial spy. It is a question whether the young America of prodigals and truants who fled the boredom or tyranny of the theocratic communities, carrying the seeds of what is America now, possessed the spirit of English or of absolute liberty. They fared abroad, perhaps, not only because the land and its promise lured them, but because they would not live at home. Such co-operation as they learned, consequently, they learned because the land exacted it, on the penalty of death. Where the land was kinder, or had been conquered, they were as dogmatic, as imperious, as intolerant, as their fathers. Even if America were "all one prairie, swept by a universal tornado," it is not the prairie which compels uniformities, nor the tornado that fixes the grammar of assent in which is parsed the modern American mind. Prairie and tornado, when they cease to be mere material environment that must be tamed and humanized and become circumstances of life that may be understood and expressed, liberate and diversify. Main Street is not of their making but of man's.

For the secularization of Calvinism merely shifted the seat of authority from the revealed word of God in the Bible to the no less sacred word of the Fathers in the Constitution. The pattern of government which this provided reproduced itself like Royce's maps from nation to state, from state to city, with a uniform rigidity over which the communism and Catholicism that Mr. Santayana contrasts with English liberty

have no advantage. The dogmas of the Constitution acquired a holiness no less sinister than
Mr. Santayana calls Jehovah's—after, that is,
the southern minority, which now composes "the
solid South," had been coerced into a surrender
of its own type of absolutism; and the negroes,
a dissimilar race compelled to live in an inferior
and degraded state both North and South, were
endowed with the privilege of a freedom which
has rendered this state secure for them.

There is a polarity rather than an interaction
between the sanctity of the political dogma, with
its correlates in the sameness and rigidity of the
political pattern, and those compulsions of the
mass and coercions of business which in America
are observed to snuff out personality by the
shaping of men according to the "national orthodoxy of work and progress." The former is as
absolute as ever any churchly dogma was, and
becomes more so with the thinning and attrition
of churchly differences. The latter is relative,
flexible, varying from area to area, and within
the framework of industrial organization from
industry to industry. It is in the latter, not the
former, that coöperative liberty sometimes occurs, occurs because in the latter lies the impact
and concentration of diverse liberties which are
like to be equal in power and need, and must
therefore adjust themselves to one another or die,

both. There exists, it is true, within the latter, a caste that is consecrated to the infallibility of the political dogma and the political forms which utter it. The caste have always been the beneficiaries of these, whether through the public land grants of the beginning or the tariff of these latter days. They naturally seek to maintain this benefaction in a country which industry has converted from a nation of individuals into a nation of classes, by invoking, as in the war upon the labor union, the dogma of absolute individual liberty where it can no longer exist, where it must become coöperative liberty if it is to be liberty at all. Notwithstanding, industry compels coöperation and it is doubtful whether this class can have its way. Its way is not the way of English liberty and never was; yet it has given the pitch to the religion of God while that mattered, and set the key for the religion of the State which began to matter from the moment when the English Colonials agreed to conceive themselves as a sovereign state dedicated to life, liberty, and the pursuit of happiness.

III

The corporate personality which was defined by the philosophy of natural rights of the Declaration of Independence and was embodied in

the form of federal government established by
the Constitution, is essentially an artificial thing.
It rests on no foundation of immemorial custom
or consanguineous tradition. It is a thing made,
not grown, and it is that by virtue of whose existence the American most specifically distin-
guishes himself from other human associations,
regardless of what other qualities compose and
designate him, or how profoundly. Englishmen
or Frenchmen think of themselves in their natures rather than their political institutions;
Americans think of themselves in their political
institutions. The consequences are inestimable.
For it is a trick of the mind that its inventions,
that serve like names in this differentiating fashion, shall become centers for the accretion of
values which turn them from engines of service
into objects of adoration. They get transformed, instruments hypostatized, idols of the
forum, market-place and cave. The moving life
of the nation may glide from under them, carrying their worshippers into new and unexpected
relations and responsibilities. But the idols will
then grow more precious as they are felt to recede, and the urge to make their adoration universal will become more imperative with their
remoteness. The "Americanism" with which self-
conscious, polite America is challenging the
worship of the world is an idol of this nature and

status. It is not the expression of present needs and future satisfactions. It is the concretion of satisfactions and privileges remembered, when the land was wilder than it is, and its people needier, cheerier and more gainful.

This, I think, is the Americanism Mr. Santayana best knew and now interprets. If the liberty which he attributes to it is in his regard an inheritance, the most precious America possesses from the English ancestor, the intense idealism about matter of the descendant is an endowment or an imposition from the American soil. Mr. Santayana's characterization of this soil is rather simple, rather scanty. He sees it as all one prairie, monotonous, uniform, empty, the chief natural features continentally spaced, so that the land does not invite one to take root, but to wander. The differences between North and South and East and West, between what is intrinsic in New England and what is intrinsic in Kansas, or Virginia, or California, or Wisconsin, are ignored; the diversification of identical stocks by river and hill, by table-land and plain, are ignored or regarded as trivial and indifferent beside the vast monotony and overruling emptiness of the midland spaces. These are the determinants of the American character. They "bring a sort of freedom to both soul and body." They induce in the soul a moral emptiness to mate the material one, for space is freedom to move, and where life has failed to take root, "where men and houses are easily moved about, and no one, almost, lives where he was born or believes what he has been taught," no tradition can continue, no customs sustain a community, no past compel with authority. These things slip away from men even as they move. They face bare Nature, unassisted but also untrammeled by the past. She becomes a challenge and a task, the material for any experiment, evoking and strengthening initiative, originality, efficiency, directness and imagination. The conquest, exploitation and use of Nature becomes the chief, the only, deep preoccupation of the American. He faces her present starkness in the hope of her future bounty. He becomes "an idealist working on matter," a moral materialist, hence, by force of circumstances; practical, worldly, helpful, efficient; full of vitality, obsessed by the optimistic assumption that "the more existence the better"; measuring life and the values of life, like a fisherman his haul, in terms of quantity and indifferent as to quality. It is these traits that the soil has evoked and fixed in him·and in these it has made him young, for it has required him to be "chiefly occupied with his immediate environment in terms of reactions . . . inwardly prompted, spontaneous and full of vivacity and self-trust." Experience has not yet brought on the sobriety of recollected failure and the chastening of emotions from which maturity and age eventuate; and in whose harmony and self-restraint is the joy of a true moral idealism. Only these can determine whether the American will remain forever an "idealist working on matter" or shall become a lover of the life of reason.

The argument is plausible and seductive. I cannot, however, state it without disturbing monitions from all the unmentioned attributes of the American scene and the unregarded diversities of the American peoples. Even the imperturbable, stoic Indians had not this unity of culture and type which Mr. Santayana assigns to transplanted Europeans and their descendants, and the period of the Indian's sojourn upon the American continent was to the Indian's advantage. Why should its emptiness and monotony not have evoked from them the same qualities it elicited from the Europeans? Why should North and South have become so different in speech, in memories, and if you please, in hope, even before the Civil War? May it not be that the America which Mr. Santayana has in mind is a very narrow America, an America of only a single one of its many types? He has seen America, so far as I know, from only three cen-

ters, along a narrow latitude—from Boston,
from Chicago, from San Francisco. The men and
women with whom he could have had anything
more than very superficial contact at these centers
are prevailingly of the same stock, the same class,
the same interest and hope. They are the build-
ers of the West, whose money or parentage was
of the East, the pioneers of the frontier, the heirs
and the bearers of the genteel tradition across
the continent. It is a tradition that has relaxed
along the westward way, so that in a progress
from Boston to San Francisco one moves from
the place of agonized conscience to a place where
civilization is on a holiday. But I doubt whether
this relaxation is the effect of the land alone and
not far more the effect of its mastery. There are
Flagellantes and devout Calvinists in California
also. The bitterness of a cult and the poverty of
a culture are alike dispelled by prosperity and
abundance. Whether in Europe or America,
pioneering, hardship and insecurity of life in the
wilderness are ever accompanied by intense faith
and proportionate intolerance. Leisure, ease, and
freedom of a wilderness subdued and a community
safeguarded are accompanied by a relaxation of
faith and a secular tolerance. What has Americanized Catholicism in the United States may
as well be the prosperity of the average Catholics
as the irrelevance of its doctrine to the necessi-

ties of the frontier. Catholicism was strongest when Europe was most barbarous. Intolerance is still an attribute of the country and tolerance of the city.

Boston also has enjoyed, or suffered, the relaxation of the genteel tradition. But that the relaxation was due to an irrelevance and a forgetting, under the impact and compulsion of a wild nature needing to be tamed, has not the indubitability with which Mr. Santayana states it. It may be that the relaxation was the effect of a compenetration and enrichment of the traditional Calvinism with the economic abundances and secular refinement of a life thereby set free from drudgery and fear, and rising hence into that enjoyment of happy and ordered living of which this is the prerequisite and condition. For I do not observe anywhere in America the passing of Puritanism by displacement and forgetting. On the contrary, Mr. Mencken and Mr. Sherman remind us that it is everywhere compellingly present, challenged, invoked, rebelled against, compromised with, lived, renounced, undergoing such a transformation as before the Reformation Catholicism was undergoing at the hands of the humanists, and for much the same reason.

Its case is not that of a memory fading before the iridescence of a welling life, and not from it springs the duplexity and essential contradiction of the American scene, "the curious alternation and irrelevance as between week-days and Sabbaths, between American ways and American opinions." These are born of the strain between its mobile expanding economy and its rigid political pattern, compelling it to develop new organs and instrumentalities of government instead of adapting old ones. But I do not discern in the cultural background of the United States anything discontinuous with its cultural present, like a new species springing from a new soil. There is a change in the accent, but no diminution of the content, of the past. An increase, rather.

The fashion, hence, which Mr. Santayana follows of treating the intellectual efflorescence of New England, about the middle of the nineteenth century, as a conclusion rather than a beginning, seems to me very dubious. "New England," he writes, "had an Indian Summer of the mind; and an agreeable reflective literature showed how brilliant that russet and yellow season could be. There were poets, historians, orators, preachers, most of whom had studied foreign literatures and had traveled; they demurely kept up with the times; they were universal humanists. But it was all a harvest of leaves; these worthies had an expurgated and

barren conception of life; theirs was the purity
of sweet old age. Sometimes they made attempts
to rejuvenate their minds by broaching native
subjects; they wished to prove how much
matter for poetry the new world supplied, and
they wrote 'Rip Van Winkle,' 'Hiawatha,' or
'Evangeline'; but the inspiration did not seem
much more American than that of Swift or
Ossian or Chateaubriand.   These cultivated
writers lacked native roots and fresh sap because the American intellect itself lacked them.
Their culture was half a pious survival, half an
intentional acquirement; it was not the inevitable flowering of a fresh experience. Later there
have been admirable analytic novelists who have
depicted American life as it is, but rather bit-
terly, rather sadly; as if the joy and the illusion
of it did not inspire them, but only an abstract
interest in their own art. If any one, like Walt
Whitman, penetrated to the feelings and images
which the American scene was able to breed out
of itself, and filled them with a frank and broad
afflatus of his own, there is no doubt that he misrepresented the conscious minds of cultivated
Americans; in them the head as yet did not belong to the trunk."

Replace in this passage New England by
Italy, or Poland, or Bohemia, or Greece, or Ireland, or Jewry, and you have, item for item, the

literary anatomy of resurgent and awakened nationalism everywhere in Europe—the transla-
tion and romantic imitation of foreign thought
and foreign manners; the superiority to the formal tradition at home; the conscious, learned
closet literature on native themes; the turn toward a didactic realism regarding the native
scene; the emergence of masters of the people's
idiom like Whitman, and their repudiation by
the cultivated; the multiplication of such masters, the babel of themes and interests, until the
national life gets steadily set in direction and intent, and literature takes on expressive perti-
nency.

This is the very springtide adventure of the
national mind, freed and made self-conscious by
prosperity—or sorrow—and seeking first to show
that it is as good, as competent and as refined as
its longer established neighbors, and secondly, to
search out, among the many forms established
in excellence and authority which the world offers, the form of communication and self-utter-
ance most congenial to its own nature. It has
ever begun by adventuring abroad for its silken
garmenting, spurning its homespun, whether in
Chaucer's day or in Longfellow's. And it seems
ever to have ended by improving the native
weave through admixture and combination of the
foreign. So it was in New England. The na-

tional consciousness long absorbed by the reju-
venating immediacies of nature, had finally, by
mastering them, established itself in a degree of
unwonted security and leisure. Looking about,
it beheld new and unsuspected perspectives, and
to the fascination of the foreign, the old and
elaborated and tried, it succumbed. Like every
nouveau riche it was bound to adorn itself with
the traditional trappings of cultural excellency
and to surround itself with the goods traditionally established in approval. At the same time
it would not abate a jot or tittle of its own claim
to dignity and power. It surveyed its world and
found it good and approved itself as the good
world's maker, like little Jack Horner in the
nursery corner proclaiming his moral superiority
with every plum he extracted from the Christ-
mas pie.

Such was the spirit of New England about
the middle of the nineteenth century, such
is the spirit of the whole of America to-day.
On the western corner of the Boston Public
Garden, facing the church of which he was long
the pastor, there is a statue of William Ellery
Channing, set up not many years ago. The inscription, taken from his sermons, is superlative,
and it fits Gopher Prairie, Minnesota, or Madison, Wisconsin, as closely as it fits Boston. "I
see," it announces, "the marks of God in the

heaven and in the earth, but how much more in a liberal intellect, in magnanimity, in unconquerable rectitude, in a philanthropy which forgives every wrong and which never despairs of the cause of Christ and human virtue. I do and must reverence human nature. I bless it for its kind affections. I honor it for its achievements in science and in art and still more for its examples of heroic and saintly virtue. These are marks of divine origin and the pledges of a celestial inheritance. I thank God that my own lot is bound up with that of the human race."

Mr. Santayana has firmly understood and perfectly expressed the public sentiment which this inscription utters. He has observed that it is "the traditional orthodoxy, the belief, namely, that the universe exists and is governed for the sake of man or of the human spirit." The liberalism that came with leisure and knowledge and prosperity has, he considers, left the orthodoxy untouched. He would not conceive that stated as Channing stated it, so innocently, naïvely, ridiculously arrogant, it breathes itself the very breath of liberalism. For illiberalism does not reside in illusion regarding the importance of mankind, but in illusion regarding the importance of a particular class of men; liberalism does not consist in the surrender of the pathetic fallacy, but of its narrow or intolerant implications. Calvinism, like other forms of salvational religion, like Judaism, is through its doctrine of special election at the core illiberal. It separates mankind forever into the damned and the saved, and it rewards the self-abasement which is the prerequisite to salvation with a predestined eternal supremacy. Its progression from Edwards to Channing, or for that matter, to Royce, has not been a process of displacement or attrition so much as a process of expansion and assimilation. This inscription from the back of Channing's niche is Calvinism without the self-abasement and without the exclusiveness. It is the doctrine of predestination and election, extended to the whole of mankind, with some reservations, inevitable in the nature of the case, and altogether unconscious, in favor of New England as a vantage point: "I thank God that my own lot is bound up with that of the human race!"

This sentiment is not unnatural to a people who, mastering Nature swiftly and effectively, were looking upon their work and finding it good. Past achievement, present effort and future hope all argued election and predestination. Isolation, and detachment from the problems and perplexities of Europe made Europe a scene and America a spectator who might and did thank God that he was not as other men. But Europe mattered to America also significantly;

significantly as a collection of cultural results, not a political and economic process. In comparison with the latter, the associations of men engaged in continental economic enterprise and bound together and distinguished as a nation by the one peculiar idea and organization known as the United States of America felt themselves to be the wards of a superior and manifest destiny. Persons of so fortunate and victorious a history could not fail to be impervious to the starkness of materialism, or most expressive in the pathetic fallacies of idealism, which Mr. Santayana aptly calls the "higher superstition." But the peoples of Europe, although they had been long disciplined by suffering and sobered by disillusion, were in no better case. If the nineteenth century was not the time and America not a place where "pure truth" could be sought, neither do any other time and place seem to have been. At least the nineteenth century attained fully, without the promptings of need and the urge of faith, in America as well as in Europe, such a knowledge of nature and man as is without precedent and without parallel in the laborious and dreamful history of the human mind. That this knowledge was put to social uses, and set in a hopeful vision of all things whose source and center were the heart of man rather than the heart of things, can hardly be made a reproach by a thinker who realizes so profoundly as does Mr. Santayana that "even under the most favorable circumstances no mortal can be asked to seize the truth in its wholeness or at its center." Should it not suffice that, after millennia of subjectivity and anthropocentric bias, men were able anywhere to approach Nature and their own foregone conclusions with a question? Could they have done it, any more than the Greeks could, without the freedom which prosperity established, and the animal assurance that a world interrogated would not reply with an insult or a blow?

IV

The academic environment, where alone this question was conspicuously raised, was the meeting place, and remains the meeting place the world over, of the old and the new. Mr. Santayana's account of its limitations, its prepossessions and perversities is undoubtedly correct, but I can not believe that they are important or especially American. For better or for worse, philosophers are professors, and if "the tendency to gather and to breed them in universities does not belong to ages of free and humane reflection," if "it is scholastic and proper to the middle ages and to Germany," it must be remembered that this tendency crystallized into an

institution in the age of free and humane reflection which Mr. Santayana most admires and that
the regimentation of thinkers into schools is the
work of the very Plato and Aristotle whose
"charming myths and civilized ethics" he would
have the philosopher who must teach for a living
expound to his pupils. It is not the gathering of
philosophers in schools that betrays philosophy:
it is the regimentation of opinion when they are
gathered, the prostitution of free thought to religious dogma and political expediency, the sub-
jection of the spirit of free inquiry to the vested
interests of the mind and the pocket. These
convert the thinker into the lay priest, the lover
of truth into the lackey of prejudice. And even
that danger it is better for the philosopher to
live with, than to live alone. If his thinking is
only a soliloquy and never a communication, he
may be a god, but never a man, and the chances
are all against the likelihood that, wandering, as
Mr. Santayana would have him, "alone like the
rhinoceros," he can escape resembling one.

In Harvard College the secularization of Calvinism came to pass earlier, more easily and
more gracefully than in New England as a
whole, and far more radically and honestly than
the secularization of the evangelical Christian-
isms that dominated the various colleges of the
protestant countries of Europe. The same com-

pulsions of a wilderness needing to be mastered
or submitted to which converted Calvinism from
a doctrine of election through self-abasement to
a doctrine of election through self-assertion, converted the traditional architects of educational
discipline in the colleges into a sort of educational
town meeting, where every subject had one vote
and no privileges and the student might elect it
according to his inertia, need or taste. It is this,
and not, as Mr. Santayana thinks, the exigencies of the teacher's task, that generated that
peculiarity of mind and temper which pervaded
the Harvard of his riper years and which he so
well describes. The teacher's task is the same
everywhere, in Oxford or Berlin or Paris as in
Cambridge. But its background in Cambridge
was a new kind of academic life in the making,
which demanded courage, experiment and faith
in the prosperous outcome of an adventure without precedent, a game with rules as yet unen-
acted. Against these concrete uncertainties of
daily life, the cosmic certainties of the comfortable ideals of the compensatory tradition were
security and insurance. They gave the animal-
darkness of living enterprise such light of thought
as it could endure, and the one was as natural
to the picture as to the other.

The world which an American student was
preparing for was a world in which everything

was in process, a world without traditions, standards, conventions or hereditary classes. It was a
world all frontier. Everywhere, in the cities of
the East as well as the plains of the West, there
were the confrontation, impact and consequent
crumbling at the edges of all the racial groupings, all the national and religious associations
of Europe. Men and women, fixed in the habit
of thought and action by the smooth customs and
intimate conventions of ancient place and long
forgotten time of the homeland, found themselves one day, thinking and acting all irrele-
vantly, as in a vacuum, their own society seeming
dissolved and lost, and no community present or
formed in which they felt at home. America
thus tended to become in the heart of its population a congeries of individuals, living each on his
own, somewhat distrustful, tense, alert, but
hopeful.

Against this process of comminution, and
imposed upon it somehow from above, rather
than growing out of it, there were the uniform
pattern of the political institution and the rigidity of the political dogma; there was the free
public school, which had replaced the church as
the transmitter of tradition and the custodian
and teacher of true doctrine; and there was the
ultimate and inescapable coercion of the automatic machine and the new industrial and finan-

cial economy which, with the machine's coming, began to displace the old. The academic world was the barometer of this situation. In a society then so atomized as the American, communities and companies formed and faded like smoke clouds in the sky; nothing was fixed, nothing inevitable; only the common, the formal, could be cleaved to, as a foothold against the universal atomizing flux. One element of this common doctrine has been, for all the peoples, the "higher superstition" and its vogue in the universities is a true reflection of the needs and will of American life. The other element, and a far more important one, has been the democratic dogma, with its institutional rigidity, its agrarian and legalistic individualism and the remaining items of its implication rendered false or irrelevant by the shifting of the economic base and technique of the national life. Outside of these certainties there was no telling what bit of curious knowledge or apparently irrelevant lore might not become the saving item in the life and death struggle of the valiant young soul set out to win the world. The university, hence, must supply everything, from the proprieties of philosophy and politics, to the eccentricities of philology or the superfluities of the fine arts. It must prepare its young men not to fill a station which awaits them, ready-made, but to make themselves

a station which they could fill. This is what
Harvard only aspired to when Santayana was a
student there. This, I think, is what Harvard
thought it was accomplishing when he had become a teacher there.

It was inevitable that an academy so inspired
should be wide rather than deep, and that formal
education should be activist, technical and unordered, a challenge and evocation of powers
rather than "the transmission of a particular
moral and intellectual tradition." The tradition
was too reassuring and too pervasive to require
intentional transmitting; its pertinent living
realities, moreover, were the orthodoxies of the
historical and political "sciences," and in them it
was transmitted and transmitted intact. The
philosophers, hence, were in a position much
freer and more daring than either the historians
or the political economists. If "their sense of
social responsibility was acute, because they
were consciously teaching and guiding the community," and if "it made no less acute their
moral loneliness, isolation, and forced self-reli-
ance" it was precisely not because "they were like
clergymen without a church, and not only had
no common philosophic doctrine to transmit but
were expected not to have one," but because in
the character which American society then owned
and does still to some degree own, the philosopher

was as foot-loose as every one else, and had like
every one else to justify his being by the competency of his doing; he had to "make good."
Nor at the time does he seem to have desired
anything different. That he could, like Santayana or James or Royce, be at one and the
same time a genuine philosopher and a popular
professor is the sign that the incompatibility of
these two rôles of which Mr. Santayana com-
plains, is more adventitious than necessary: the
progenitor of the species was after all the Socrates of Mr. Santayana's admiration. The result was that excellence of the Harvard school
of philosophy which in spite of his modest depre-
cations Mr. Santayana signalizes. It was "a
vital unit and coöperative in its freedom. There
was a general momentum in it, half institutional,
half moral, a single troubled, noble, exciting life.
Every one was laboring with the contradiction
he felt in things, and perhaps in himself; all were
determined to find some honest way out of it, or
at least to bear it bravely. It was a fresh morn-
ing in the life of reason, cloudy but brightening."

It is good to recall how, of this vital unit, co-
operative in its freedom, of personalities so
unique and insights so noble and so contrary,
Santayana was one, and the peer of any.

V

The discussion of James and Royce by the
last survivor of the great school brings together
in a fashion vivid and touching and beautiful
the diversified spirit of its oneness, the uncom-
promised singularity of each member of that
high fellowship. There is neither need nor service here to expound and review the differences
between Mr. Santayana and his colleagues, and
to resume his criticisms, profound or wise or mis-
chievous or uncomprehending, of idealism and
pragmatism, or his harder, less urbane, somewhat
contemptuous judgment of the new realism.
These have been often stated and are well known,
and the perfection of their form adds an esthetic,
not a logical, value to their content. Nor is anything changed in Mr. Santayana's method. He
still restates the alien doctrine in the light not of
its own premise and the signification of its own
terms, but of his own view as critic. He still
makes the same assumption that such a shift of
the premises does not put the argument beside
the point, that it does not, like the "higher superstition," convert inquiry into an exercise in the
grammar of assent, that it is not in its own
turn the arguing of a foregone conclusion and
the parsing over again of the ancient premise of
all doctrine, *I prefer to believe*. Take as an

instance, the discussion of James's ideas regarding the will to believe: "In some cases," Mr. Santayana interprets, "faith in success could nerve us to bring success about, and so justify itself by its own operation. This is thought typical of James at his worst—a worst in which there is always a good side. Here again psychological observation is used with the best intentions to hearten oneself and other people; but the fact observed is not at all understood, and a moral twirl is given to it which (besides being morally questionable) almost amounts to falsifying the fact itself. Why does the belief that you can jump a ditch help you to jump it? Because it is a symptom of the fact that you *could* jump it, that your legs were fit and that the ditch was two yards wide and not twenty. A rapid and just appreciation of these facts has given you your confidence, or at least has made it reasonable, manly and prophetic; otherwise you would have been a fool and got a ducking for it. Assurance is contemptible and fatal unless it is self-knowledge. If you had been rattled you might have failed, because that would have been a symptom of the fact that you were out of gear; you would have been afraid because you trembled, as James at his best proclaimed. You would never have quailed if your system had been reacting smoothly to its opportunities, any more than you would titter and see double if you were not intoxicated. . . . Nor is the moral suggestion here less unsound. What is good is not the presumption of power but the possession of it: a clear head, aware of its resources, not a fuddled optimism, calling up spirits from the vasty deep. Courage is not a virtue, said Socrates, unless it is also wisdom. Could anything be truer both of courage in doing and of courage in believing? But it takes tenacity, it takes *reasonable* courage, to stick to scientific insights such as this of Socrates or that of James about the emotions; it is easier to lapse into the traditional manner, to search natural philosophy for miracles and moral lessons, and in morals prefer, in the reasoned expression of preference, to splash about without a philosophy."

Those who recall the passage in *The Sentiment of Rationality* on which these sentences are commentary will perceive at once how it is parodied, and—the observation is unavoidable—degraded. An unwonted and momentous situation is made over into a commonplace one; an issue of life and death into one of walking dryshod or getting a ducking; an abyss is converted into a ditch, a terrible leap into a commonplace jump. The propulsive emotional crisis, the ab-

sence or impossibility of any basis competent for
inference are converted into their opposites. The
process of the self-confirmation of the act of
faith that creates its own verification is displaced
by the prior guarantee in observation of this
verification. Prospect and change are declared
to be really retrospect and fixity; you *have*
jumped the ditch because you *could*. The whole
premise of the argument has been shifted and the
contrary conclusion drawn from the contrary
premise. The risk, on which courage is postulated, the conception of faith as the willingness,
in James's words, "to act in a cause the prosperous issue of which is *not* certified to us in ad-
vance," or as the "courage weighted with responsibility—such courage as the Nelsons and
Washingtons never failed to show after they
had taken everything into account that might
tell against their success and made every provision to minimize disaster," these are ruled out.
After much brave protestation, the game is made
a game with loaded dice after all, made just what
in James's hypothesis it absolutely was not. In
effect, the argument does not refute, it contra-
dicts. Mr. Santayana's philosophy runs parallel
with those of his colleagues but does not meet
them. The same heaven arches over them, whose
shifting iridescence they alike give back; they are
fed by the same springs and they water the same

lands and are by them muddied, and that is all. They touch sometimes, but mingle never, and perhaps never could.

It is this mingling of the same earth and sky in their separate streams that renders them alike American. Neither Santayana could escape the bondage of the "two different responsibilities," that of "describing things as they are, and that of finding them propitious to certain preconceived human desires." For the life of reason is no less such a desire, and for all its obscuration no less pervasive, and for all its urbanity no less capable of becoming a dogma and generating a religion, than the "higher superstition." The adventure after the "good life" was undertaken by all three alike, under a similar impulse and in a similar atmosphere. That what each found should have been different is not without its implication of the nature of things, or of the condition of the intellectual life in the United States. And that one kind of life only should be called a good life, and that of a fashion arising not from the soil of present life, but from a memory and estimate of life long gone, that perhaps is most romantic and American of all.

Of the relations of James and James's thought to this America, Mr. Santayana says very little. He remarks how essentially different and other James appeared to the academic and social community in which he dwelt, how he was a liberal—"one of those elder Americans still disquieted by the ghost of tyranny, social and ecclesiastical," but nothing more. He ignores his militant love of peace, so essentially American, his reformist spirit, so characteristic of New England. His preoccupation is entirely with James's temperament and philosophy. These he sums up as "a romantic mind soaked in agnosticism, conscious of its own habits and assuming an environment the exact structure of which can never be observed"; the conception of radical empiricism and pragmatism as methods, the analysis of belief, the notion of pure experience, the analysis of truth, and the other spokes in the wheel of James's thought are really treated as radiations from this central hub. Consequently, James's greatness accrues to him as a psychologist, not as a philosopher. Philosophy was to him, in Mr. Santayana's estimation, not a "consolation and a sanctuary in life which would have been unsatisfying without it," but "a maze in which he found himself wandering," and he was trying to find his way out of the maze. But this philosophy, Mr. Santayana fails to recognize, was the verbiage of the schools; it was not the way out or the brave seeing of the contradiction in things and in oneself which he as bravely celebrated in his description of the Harvard school.

Yet, to the American aspect of this contradiction in things and men James was a philosopher most sensitive. In his training and contacts he was essentially more cosmopolitan than either of his colleagues; his philosophy was nevertheless an insight into the everlasting springs of this contradiction, flowing so much more freely, into channels so much less artificial in America than in Europe. He had a greater natural kinship with America's spontaneous life and he envisaged in a pertinent metaphysical premise the whole unbalanced and shifting structure of the changing American economy; the atomism and fluidity of American society; the democratic dogma; and, most famously and influentially, the tenacious experimentalism, the swift courage, the stark faith of men to put life and property and opinion to the proof of adventure into the unknown wilderness toward whatever "good life" nature suggested or calculation advised.

In Royce's thinking the same influences are present, but not freely. Between them and his vision there is interposed the veil of the genteel tradition, and its unity and texture impart to them a false solidity. He is not, like James, looking at the tradition as well as the thing, and evaluating the tradition also. He is looking at the thing, certainly, persistently, and looking at it *through* the tradition. Hence a certain liturgi-

cal unction and obscurity which pervades Royce's
thought. He viewed everything, Mr. Santayana
says, in relation to something else, and this something contained invariably an element sad and
troublesome, out of which the thing under view,
if good, arises by a sort of Hegelian implication.
His proof of the existence of God is his demonstration of the reality of error; his assurance of
the reality of the good was his experience of the
power of evil. He argued, in effect, in his own
special way the foregone conclusions of the
"higher superstition." His philosophy was all
compensatory. By translating Calvinism into
epistemological terms, by imparting to the dialectic method of Hegel the earnestness, eloquence
and voluble passion of his own temperament and
scene, he gave the genteel tradition a new pattern and an added content. This was not logical.
He had, it is true, a reputation for logic and
loved the intricacies of logistics; he could, on occasion, eye to eye with Spinoza, see things under
the aspect of eternity. But "there was no clearness in his heart." In him the intellect, which
Mr. Santayana regards as the "faculty of seeing
things as they are," was dimmed and distorted
by the passion for seeing things as we want
them to be. Nevertheless, the hardness of the
nature of things, its pang and poison, troubled
Royce. He had a reverence for what hurts: "In

so far as God was the devil . . . devil worship
was true religion." Life and the good of life are
the struggle between good and evil, and the
struggle can not be unless evil exists, the peer of
good. The proof of this was evident in daily
routine as well as Hegelian logic. Royce "had
always experienced and seen about him a grop-
ing, burdened, mediocre life; he had observed
how fortune is continually lying in ambush for
us, in order to bring good out of evil and evil
out of good. In his age and country all was
change, preparation, hurry, material achievement; nothing was an old and sufficient possession. . . . The whole scene was filled with acts
and virtues which were merely useful or remedial.
The most pressing arts, like war and forced labor, presuppose evil, work immense havoc, and
take the place of greater possible goods. The
most indispensable virtues, like courage and industry, do likewise. But these seemed in Royce's
world the only honorable things." Thus the
grappling with nature of which so much of
American life consists was converted into a standard of life, and given such grace and distinction
as clothing it in the decent garment of the genteel tradition might impart. In this lay Royce's
personal conscience, and it carried him beyond
his Hegelian ethics, as his protest against the
sinking of the Lusitania showed. By training

and technique a Hegelian, by implication a solipsist, this conscience of his, which "added a deep, almost remorseful unrest to his hard life," carried him beyond Hegelism, making his God real, and begging the gratuity of another life in the immortal society of his friends. All in all, Royce "resembled some great-hearted medieval peasant visited by mystical promptings, whom the monks should have adopted and allowed to browse among their theological folios. . . . His was a gothic and scholastic spirit, intent on honoring God in systematic works, like the coral insect or the spider; eventually creating a fabric that in its homely intricacy and fullness arrested and moved the heart, the web of it was so vast, and so full of mystery and yearning."

It may be inferred from Mr. Santayana's treatment of both James and Royce that the fullness of the new world influence was not manifest in them. To him their insight was a mingling of tradition and actualities, with tradition more than a little dominant. In the later contemporary movements of philosophy in America the relationships are, however, reversed. Tradition is either passing or forgotten. He sees the younger professors of philosophy as more like engineers or doctors or social reformers than clergymen or schoolmasters. Religion has ceased to signify anything momentous for them. They

are no longer so eloquent and apostolic as professors of philosophy used to be; instead, "very
professional in tone and conscious of their *Fach*,"
a special craft in the academic industry. The
younger American professor of philosophy is a
person with an education "more pretentious than
thorough; his style is deplorable; social pressure
and his own great eagerness have condemned
him to overwork, committee meetings, early marriage, premature authorship and lecturing two or
three times a week under forced draught. He
has no peace in himself, no window open to a
calm horizon, and in his heart perhaps little taste
for mere scholarship or pure speculation. Yet,
like the plain soldier staggering under his clumsy
equipment, he is cheerful; he keeps his faith in
himself and his allotted work, puts up with being
toasted only on one side, remains open-minded,
whole-hearted, appreciative, helpful, confident of
the future of goodness and of science. In a
word, he is a cell in that teeming democratic
body; he draws from its warm, contagious activities the sanctions of his own life, and less consciously the spirit of his philosophy."

The marching front of this spirit is to be found
in pragmatism and new realism. The former is
a confusion of mind which converts truth, the
vision of all things under the form of eternity,
ever beyond the reach of psychology, into the

psychological doctrine of the relation of signs
to things signified, interpreting this relation in
terms of contiguity and succession. The latter
is a standing on its head of the traditional German idealism. This replaced things by consciousness; the new realism replaces consciousness by things. It relieves "an overtaxed and
self-infected generation" by "abolishing a prerequisite to the obvious, and leaving the 'obvious
to stand alone." It democratizes reality by re-
ducing everything to the same status and making
it equally accessible to everybody. "The young
American is thus reassured: his joy in living and
learning is no longer chilled by the contempt
which idealism used to cast on nature for being
imaginary and on science for being intellectual."
Both the contemporary schools thus reflect the
atmosphere of America, and in two ways. First,
in that "it has accelerated and rendered fearless
the disintegration of conventional categories.
. . . In the second place, the younger cosmopolitan America has favored the impartial assem-
blage and mutual confrontation of all sorts of
ideas. It has produced, in intellectual matters,
a sort of happy watchfulness and insecurity."
And this is how migration to the new world has
affected philosophical ideas.

Which may be so. But I doubt whether even
those pragmatists and new realists who have been

curious about just such matters and have reflected on them will recognize the features of their ancestry or themselves in the portrait. "The disintegration of conventional categories," they will concede, but the new realists will insist, I think, that so far as they are concerned it is a conventional and not an American disintegration, and that the forces which operate it in America do not differ in kind, intensity or range from those in Europe. The pragmatists will concede the total implication of the description, but will declare that Mr. Santayana has altogether failed to grasp its character and import. This failure is perhaps at base emotional rather than intellectual. Mr. Santayana has always manifested a certain blindness to the ideas of change and time and flux in their intrinsicality and inwardness, and a certain imperviousness to the meaning of the categories and concepts which have grown out of them, and the new philosophic technique which they have generated. Preoccupied with the eternal, the static, the immutable, as Plato and Aristotle and Spinoza have formulated these in ethics and physics and psychology, he has invariably translated the studies of the temporalists into the language of the eternalists, substituting these incommensurables for one another, with beautiful but not cogent results. With the new realists, on the other hand, he is more at home. He and they have the same devotion and speak the same language. They also are eternalists, preoccupied with "the" unchanging structure of things. They are, however, so preoccupied, not because they recognize change and acquiesce in insecurity, but because they deny change and, fearing, resent insecurity. That they have "abolished the prerequisite to the obvious" is a sign of this denial and resentment. This abolition is not a simplification which frees the new realist's "joy in living and learning . . . from the contempt which idealism used to cast on nature for being imaginary and on science for being didactic." On the contrary, there appears to be no joy in the neo-realist. He is as Calvinistic as his forbears. Only the incidence of the cosmic compulsion has been shifted for him. It resides no longer in the immutable decrees of a transcendental God, but in the immutable architectonic of a nature whose laws operate by logistical implication and whose providence is didactic without being altogether personal. Thus, together with the denial of a prerequisite to the obvious goes the establishment and cultivation of security, the relaxation of watchfulness. It is an attenuation of the "higher superstition," but it is the higher superstition still. It is the modern scholasticism, the scholasticism of science converted from a method of inquiry into a process of affirmation, from the logic of experiment to the logic of assertion. Its social inspiration is to be sought in financial industrialism, with the regimentation, precision, inevitability, of the automatic machine in shop and factory, and in the similar qualities more refined in the mathematics of accounting in bank and office. It is unrelated to the sentiment, experience and aspiration of the migration to the new world. That has still not reached expression in philosophy. It is as yet vocal in poetry alone.

VI

So much, then, for Mr. Santayana's resolution of the puzzle of America. It is complementary rather than parallel to those of his predecessors and fellows in the field, dealing with an inward aspect of American character and opinion too withdrawn and elusive for any but a familiar friend to touch without distorting or to interpret without misunderstanding. It has the same narrowness and oversimplification as these others, but if it is blind to what they have seen, it is keenly sensitive to what they are blind to. Mr. Santayana is himself perhaps too deeply absorbed by the ardors and glories of the topmost turn given to life to have much sympathy for its soil or roots or branches. His study has

failed to take note of the political character of
the American being, of the overwhelming influence of the rigid identities of political pattern of
state, nation and city, or the power of the public
school as the transmitter of the national tradition and the perpetuator of the democratic
dogma, or the relation of these to the stratifying
influence of the automatic machine, or the interaction of these with the diversities of soil and
climate, race and culture which are constitutive
of the land, and the additional diversities which
are added by "the miscellany of Europe." These
seem to me at the present time to have been adjusted to one another as a tensive and unstable
equilibrium of forces rather than a coöperation
of spirits; the various movements in art or philosophy appear more truly as negations of them
or compensations for them than as their expression. What the America of the new time will
be depends altogether on how soon and how completely the unstable equilibrium of forces is converted into the coöperation of spirits, and the negations and compensations become affirmations
and expressions.

VI

HUMANISM AND THE INDUSTRIAL AGE [1]

I

THE men of the 19th century in Europe were, perhaps far more completely than any men of earlier ages, discoverers, creators, conquerors, and poets. Their science probed Nature almost to her very heart, their machines compressed space and restrained time, their arts and industries brought into being a way of life so new and so wonderful, that there was no thing in the past to set by its side, so strange and unheard of were its engines, its enterprise, its knowledge and its goods. So unprecedented were they, so unique, that it seemed to many as if the character and requirements of man's habitation had been transformed overnight and they were overcome with a sense at once of dissociation and insecurity like that of a newcomer in a foreign land. In their habits and ideals of life, even in their joy and

[1] First printed in *The New Republic*, January, 1923.

their hope, they felt suddenly at a loss. For
those did not change at once with their habitation; they remained set, adjustments to a re-
treating order of society and a lapsing economy.
It is not strange, therefore, that the men of the
19th century should so often appear to their
critics of a later generation as a breed without
happiness and without vision. How could there
be any clearness in their hearts, or any light in
their minds? They were confused by the multiplicity and tumult of their own works, by the
persistence, in spite of disarticulation, of old
habits and old thoughts, so that they were inhibited from understanding and incapacitated
from mastering their handiwork. The sensitive
were filled with revulsion, the practical with
greed; the mass could only yield themselves to
the momentum of their machines, with a sort of
blind brute faith, unchastened and perennial as
the urge of life itself, that justified events as
events came, and carried on, like an animal en-
trapped in its own burrow, without a plan and
without a purpose.

It was a century of unrest and discontent. Its
most articulate spirits were prophets of disillusion and apostles of retreat. It is hard to name
any of them—Carlyle, Newman, Ruskin, Marx,
Nietzsche, Tolstoi, Arnold, Bergson—who did
not describe civilization as a sin and offer his

doxy as a salvation. The babel of salvation, indeed, was no less a confusion than the noise of the captains of industry and the shouting. Only toward the end of the century did signs appear that the babel could be a chorus, that unrest could make a unison, and discontent a chord. Hatred of the new economy of industry, of its impersonality, its automatism, its compulsions, appeared as the common passion of classes, sects and parties. However diversified and antagonistic their loves had been—Carlyle advocated a medieval paternalism; Tolstoi a primitive Christian communism; Marx a late materialistic one; Nietzsche a superman; Newman a church, Arnold, sweetness and light; Bergson a mystical abundance of life—their hates were one. They had grown more articulate about its own intrinsic nature and deficiencies, and had come closer to a realistic perception of their own disharmony with it, whence they drew, in the formula of "the class struggle" a pattern for their discontent and for their unrest, a form. But that was all.

This unanimity of hatred and diversity of loves has passed over little modified from the 19th to the 20th century. Currently, I have been interested in two groups who challenge and denounce the age and such ideals as they discern for it. One of these groups, who are now a sort of Genro of rebellious youth, and whose sincerest Ameri-

can voice was once the brave, twisted figure of
Randolph Bourne, has no alternative ideal to present. Its spirit is disaffection, its cry: There is
no good in the institutions of modern life; they
enslave, they inflict suffering, they suffocate independence and originality; they spread the pall
of age and death on all things, but most of all on
young things—let youth go free, and freedom will
grow youth's proper ideals for youth. The other
group raises aloft a banner with an old device:
Humanism. It does envisage and cherish and
prophesy an alternative ideal, at once doctrine
and discipline. This ideal, its apostles say, has
for its roots the essential nature of man; for its
trunk the tradition of cultured living transmitted
by the generations; for its leafage, the doctrine
and discipline of this tradition, spreading to the
open weather; for its fruit, the perfections of
aristocracy—gentlemen; whose lives conform to
the standards set by Aristotle and Castiglione,
by La Rochefoucauld and Cardinal Newman.
This Humanism, and this alone, can truly save
the soul alive from the unhappy submission to
matter which is the slavish spirit of modern society, from the preoccupation with natural science, the absorption in making things to sell, and
the accumulation of money, which are its manifestations. So complete and so degraded is this
slavery that the only ideal which society regards

is the ideal of wealth, the only freedom it desires
is freedom to get rich, the only progress it appre-
hends is progress in acquisition, and the only
happiness it finds is happiness in the multiplication of possessions. With this result: The features of the community are sordid and ugly; its
rich folk are anxious and afraid, its poor discour-
aged and degraded; its arts reject what is best
for what is commonest or wildest. Its religion
has changed from a loyalty of hope to an idolatry
of despair.

But alas for the Humanism which should be
salvation from all this horror! It is unregarded
gospel. Its name is an empty sound, recalling
to the young forgotten dim events they had heard
of in dull classrooms; to the old, scraps of phrase
in ancient tongues, which they flaunt, but do not
understand. Its prophets are a diminishing
handful, preaching in a wilderness. The generation that they exhort to doctrine and to discipline is a generation that knew not Joseph. To
them its prophets seem to be no more than a
bunch of poor pedagogues, stranded safely in the
academic backwash of life, remote from reality
and without experience in living, pleading for
the security of their jobs. To them "the quarrel
between the ancients and moderns" has neither
content nor meaning. It is a forgotten quarrel,
so long have Science and Industry been the vic-

tors, so overruling has been their influence upon the minds of the times. And the light of this Science, the spokesmen of rebellious youth assert, this Science which resets all things in the order of their generation and exhibits all effects in the linkage of their causes, shows up Humanism as merely a tool of living made over into an idol of the half-dead, and the Humanists as idolators who have made of the tree of life a painted lath, of the fruits of life, fruits of fustian.

This saying has its grounds. In the perspective of history, Humanism is an adventure, not a discipline, a program of liberty, not a doctrine of regimentation. It did change from adventure to discipline and from program to doctrine, but the change was a sea-change, from a life into a recollection. When Humanism became discipline and doctrine it died. It became exactly the sort of thing against which it had been a rebellion, and it suffered the same fate. What it confronted and shattered was the regimentation of thought and conduct in the interests of the ruling church of Europe. This had filled men's hearts with the fear of death and the hope of salvation, and restricted their minds to regard only the duly authorized and authenticated tools and agencies of salvation. It had subjected them, in a word, to the other-worldly preoccupations of the theologian and the divine. In the course of time, however, the craftsmen and merchants of Europe established themselves in cities. Their number multiplied as their skills grew and differentiated. What they made they sold not only to the populace at home, but to the aristocracies abroad, and their earnings they applied to the enrichment, strengthening and easing of their common life. Their contacts, and the contacts of their upper classes through religious war and military wanderings, with peoples of other faiths and equal, or superior, powers, led them to tolerance and urbanity. Their interest in the nature and mastery of this world became more central and compelling, and in the doctrine and discipline of the church more peripheral and irrelevant. This change of heart, this true conversion of the spirit of Europe, was spread over many years. It came slowly and moved in distinct successive waves from the Mediterranean to the Baltic. Its essence was secularization, a turning of attention from the supernatural to nature, from the disingenuous service of God to the honest happiness of man.

The search for this happiness was a true liberation of mind and body. It adventured in all directions into the unknown, material and immaterial, of space, of time, of imagination. It delighted in clothing; in building; in craftsmanship and commerce; in conquest and administration;

in music, metaphysics, painting and sculpture; in language and literature. There was not a field of human endeavor which did not yield its particular glow of fresh discovery and happy use. Of these, by a lucky accident, the works of man in Greece and Rome were one, and because what they offered in beauty of form and humanity of substance could be most obviously and directly set up against the no longer savory doctrine and discipline of the church, they became the foremost symbol of the resurgence of free mind, intent on secular accomplishment and natural happiness. Classic art, classic speech, particularly Latin, classic ideas and classic ideals, became the badges of the new liberty and the new life, even in the heart of the church itself. They prevailed in the courts, the workshops, the market-places. They were adopted as the new doctrine and discipline of the schools. They were called the humanities and were treated as law-givers for mankind.

But the humanities were not in themselves law-givers. There is no force in things of the past other than the present life which regards and sustains them. Things of the past are only symbols of force. They are flags. The Humanities were the heraldry and pennants of the fecund new energies of peoples overflowing into new modes of industry and art and science and government, modes of a different pattern and springing from another root than the classics, as a factory or an army might produce values which the flag that flutters over it may stand for, but can not be. The workers may move on, the army disband, and the flag still bravely fly. It would then be representative of nothing, a past symbol, with no present ground. In the course of time wind and weather would dim its colors and unravel its weave; the stuff of it would turn to dust and be scattered to the four corners of the earth.

Not unlike, in many ways, was the story of the classics. Already before the Renaissance had definitely come to its term they too had slipped from the center to the periphery of European life. Courts and workshops and market-places ceased to regard them, and the schools became absorbed in them as formerly they had been in theology. Since education, except for the brief period of the age of Pericles, has always concerned itself with the transmission of tradition rather than the discovery of truth and with the contemplation of the past rather than the conquest of the future, the forced shift of young attention from divinity to the humanities was a matter of no importance. Institutional education was then, as now, a distraction from life, not a preparation for it, and what is momentous in the experience of the young, what rouses feeling, initiates habit and fixes character is still unrelated to what they encounter in the classroom. Whether in school or on the street, the young live a life apart. They have their own community, with its own *mores,* traditions and rules, that educate and mold them while the classroom at great pains decorates them with information —in the old days, with ribbons of Latin and pompons of Greek which on occasion they might display in public address or private talk, but which hardly ever made the slightest difference in the conduct of their lives.

From a symbol of new life to a decoration of old conventions—this is the movement of Humanism in the transition of the expansive mood of the Renaissance into the reticulated one of the 18th century, with its precise and finished formalities in manners, poetry, landscape and spirit, its whole "neo-classic" character. As a part of the texture of life, the classics were less important in that century, not more important, than in the Renaissance. The let-down in energy from the abundance of the Rebirth to the elegance of the Enlightenment, from magnificence to sufficiency, carried with it an insufficiency of sustaining life for the classics. The 18th century is relatively a period of spiritual consolidation and retrenchment, a time of reflection and accounting, of repose, order, self-analysis; consequently of disillusion and irony. It is a period of historical review and social and psychological anatomy, of formal wit and restrained laughter. Its genius, whose Renaissance protagonist was Rabelais, is Voltaire. It set commonsense against sentiment, reason against feeling and imagination, practicality against enthusiasm. It translated Homer and interpreted Aristotle, but neither what it produced nor what it interpreted was of the same stuff with what it used. In spite of its "classic" tone, it had much less in common with antiquity than the Renaissance. Its Humanism was merely of the schools, and its Humanists had ceased to be men of affairs and had become merely schoolmen. The classics remained idols of the closet, decorations of forum; they lost even the dignity and station of symbols of free life.

In the next mutation of the mood of Europe, they regained, however, what they had lost. The new mood is usually called Romanticism. It is in effect another phase of the recurrent overflow which life's energies after a time seem to accomplish against the orders and conventions which enchannel them and choke them. In this instance it began as the reaction against the regimentation which neo-classicism, in the name of the classics, practiced upon the forms of expres-

sion natural and spontaneous to changing life.
Romanticism also raised aloft the humanistic device. It also appealed to antique beauty against
present deformity and was ready, as Goethe
showed it in Faust, if need be, to ravish Helen
from hell itself. But the antiquity it appealed
to had meanwhile received a different body and
another soul. It had ceased to be an aggregation
of works of art, in letters, in stone, in paint, in
metals and jewels, each a perfection ungrounded
and isolate, without past and without future, a
Platonic idea to be loved and imitated for all time.
No, the humanities had become things fleshed in
history, set in perspectives of time and place and
circumstance, and their import had changed
with their status. The Greek past replaced the
Roman at the center of humanistic regard, and
in this new guise the humanities became once
more impedimenta of an army of rebellion, engines and banners in their battle for their new
freedom of "self-expression," "harmonious self-
development," and all the other catchwords
wherewith was designated the rejection of the
doctrine and discipline of which these same classics were the orthodox instruments and patterns.

From Winckelmann and Goethe to Swinburne
and Matthew Arnold, the end which these instruments were supposed to serve was conceived
of in identical terms. But Romanticism was

not the only aspect of the new time. Its Humanism needed to hold its precarious place against old privilege and new power, against authority, against science, against industry. Both the receding old order and the advancing new beat upon it, the tide of industry, most of all. As that gathered sweep and momentum, it was thrust farther and farther from the course of life. Finally it was again left, higher and drier than ever, in the schools. There it remains, a doctrine and a discipline, undergoing an ever quicker attrition as the backwash of social change overflows into educational policy. Its votaries are a diminishing sect, and they fight for its survival in even those poor places with a courage that does not lack its latencies of fear. Humanity, however, has passed the humanities by. As they survive in the schools, they are no longer pertinent to its concerns, and the Humanism they are supposed to conserve, to express and to transmit is unrelated to its life. Yet let no one mourn the irony of its sad fate; its priests declare that it is mankind, not Humanism, that is aborted.

Shade of Pococurante! To understand this fine flower of the humanistic spirit it is necessary only to note the bearings, in the community, of the humanists themselves. They are essential Laputans. In the security of the academic environment, they live beside life, not in it. What is dynamic in it does not touch them, and would probably consume them if it did. The things they live among are finished things, whose growth is done—things, consequently, cut off from the nourishing stream of community and conflict in aspiration and endeavor which is society, and apart from which, as the ancients well knew, nothing human can either grow or ripen. The things they live among are past things, dead things, things immortal, and possessed of that discreteness and immutability which pertain to the dead past. For only the dead can be immortal and changeless and fixed in their natures. What lives and has a future is labile and fluid. For it, there are no finalities, whether of rule or being. All is future, tentative, experimental, every mold surpassed, every category overflowed. This is why humanity has a history, and the perfections of its works are various and not one.

Minds may, however, by revulsion or decision, cut themselves off from the future. They may surrender themselves to the sole contemplation of things past and dead, that is, eternal and immortal. Such minds, minding such things, cannot overcome the illusion that the things are still forces in themselves. They cannot see that even as doctrine and discipline the humanities must have had foundations before they ever in their turn could become foundations, and that their own foundations must continue to sustain them if they are in their turn to sustain anything else. For such minds nourish the dead ghost they adore from the unknown root of their own passions and attribute the warmth it gives back to a life in the thing itself, as a country boy might, who, blowing his willow whistle, should insist that there's a bird in the hollow of his reed. This is a very distilling of sunbeams out of cucumbers, like all attribution of the energies of men to their trappings and circumstance.

II

It would be nice for *soi-disant* humanists if humanists could be made by the humanities and not by men's heritage, responding to events. Many humanists exist who have no jot or tittle of Latin or Greek, and many more champions in Greek and Latin, who have not an iota of Humanism. The humanist sect in the academies are, if their behavior be any guide, Romanticists disturbed by their own times and fleeing for refuge to antiquity. No Utopian of the future can be more bitter about what is alive in modern civilization or more coruscated with righteous indignation. But they will not try either to understand or to master it, as a true humanist would.

They reject it, as strangers here, whose home is the heaven of doctrine and discipline out of the ancient past. Language figures in that home as an effective barrier against the profane; while for the initiates to have surmounted the inert difficulty it opposes to the mind provides a pleasant sense of superiority without a real combat. That which lies beyond language is simple stuff, with form often enough adequate to it to yield beauty, and it practices besides a solicitation of massive emotion as wide in range as it is deeply, if darkly, gratifying. The doctrine and discipline of the ancient classics are a Zion in which Puritan and Satyr may lie down together and be, at ease.

And why not? If some particular portion of an unhappy and distracted generation find here sanctuary, find peace and security and pride all in one, let them take it and cleave unto it. It is their right, and none may say them nay. But can not these humanists sufficiently mitigate their Christian spirit to refrain from demanding that those of another vision and another purpose shall also adopt their special way of salvation? Must those who, like Rebellious Youth, are too sedulous to combat the present to care for sanctuary, or like the Business Man or the Laborer, are too much a part of its substance to wish or to be able to flee it, be outlawed from humanity? What reason is there to set the humanities as the *Summa* of education for all mankind?

The answer is the ultimate answer of all authoritarians to whatever challenges their privilege or authority. They invoke the old, old god out of the machine, Human Nature. Our Humanism, they say, rests on human nature; it is the inevitable perfect fruit of the humanity of mankind.

This reply is unanswerable—if true. But is it true? How shall one know and be saved? . . . Well, listen to Mr. Paul Elmer More, who is one of the American high priests of the humanist cult:

"Let a man retire into himself," he exhorts, in the course of denouncing the lovingkindness of Miss Jane Addams on behalf of an Everlasting Morality, "and examine his own motives and the sources of his self-approval and discontent. He will discover there, in that dialogue with himself, if his abstraction is complete and sincere, that his nature is not simple and single but dual, and that the consequences to him in his judgment of life and in his conduct will be of incalculable importance. He will learn with a conviction which no science or philosophy falsely so called can shake that besides the passions and wandering desires and blind impulses and the cravings for pleasure and the prod of sensations, there is something within him and a part of him, rather in some way his truer self, which controls and checks and knows and pronounces judgment, unmoved amid all motion, unchanged amid continual change, of everlasting validity above the shifting valuations of the moment."

Or again, hearken to Mr. Irving Babbitt, whose animadversions on human nature are incidental to a formulation of Humanism. He also is a dualist, half Platonic, half Kantian, seeing existence as a struggle between the Ormuzd One and the Ahriman Many: "The human mind, if it is to keep its sanity, must maintain the nicest balance between unity and plurality. . . . If man's nobility lies in his kinship to the One, he is at the same time a phenomenon among other phenomena, and only at his risk and peril neglects his phenomenal self. . . . Man is a creature who is foredoomed to one-sidedness, yet who becomes humane only in proportion as he triumphs over this fatality of his nature, only as he arrives at that measure which comes from tempering his virtues each by its opposite."

Behold, then, the human nature of the humanists current—dual and not single, composed of opposites, each pulling for itself, able to be and behave as a whole only as a balance of these opposites, with one of them, the One, somewhat predominant. And Humanism is this balance!

The continuity of this view with that combination of dialectic and mythology which used to be known in the tradition of the schools as mental philosophy is too apparent to need more than pointing out. The human nature it declares is anthropocentric and pre-Copernican. Even the Freudian censor and its unconscious, which it so much suggests, mythological as those are, are too scientific for it, and would in all likelihood be repudiated as devilish doubles. The positive sciences of man—psychology, physiology, anthropology and their like—have no authority for those who regard human nature after this fashion. As sciences they are only "so called," vain empiricisms beside a transcendental conviction to be reached by an exercise in introspection, like the conviction of the Vermont farmer who, seeing a camel for the first time, gave judgment after long contemplation, "Pshaw, there ain't no such animile!" To those, however, for whom the positive sciences do carry authority, the human nature of the humanistic sect will be a special case of the pathetic and psychologist's fallacy.

The sciences of body and mind show human nature not as a dualism, but as a true plurality; not as a balance of forces, but as an integration of dispositions; not as a mutual tempering of opposite virtues but as a coöperation of diverse powers, with the unity not outside of and op-

posed to the variety, but flowing from it and dependent on it, as the unity of a team flows from
and depends on the diversity of the players.   Its
wholesomeness is not a state of equilibrium maintained but a process of adjustment going on, in
which the body changes least and the mind most.
The homogeneity of feeling and the discreteness
of character which the different ages of recorded
time present are due to these facts; history happens because of the combination of continuity
with novelty they generate.   From the age of
Pericles to time out of mind it is a sequence of
new minds for old bodies, and in this sequence,
among the changing patterns of adjustment of
human nature to its environment, Humanism has
its place.

Now, when you set side by side the Humanism
of Erasmus and the Humanism of Goethe, or
the Humanism of Cicero and the Humanism of
Anatole France, to find out the common features
which the word should denote, you can, beyond
a quality of emotion, discover no concrete item
of such a community.   What stands out is rather
the diversity of traits in each type.   The similarity, when it exists, is subterranean and seems
more like the continuity of a biography than the
homophony of a pattern.   It is as if the energies
of man, making history, make it by finding different channels composed of different stuffs, and

the quality and timbre of what they work out are determined far more by the stuffs than by the energies that mold them.

The Greeks, to whom the original of Humanism is referred, were not humanists: they were harassed men trying to make a good life. The brief glory that was Greece was initiated in the complication of an agricultural economy with a military and commercial technology; it became effulgent as an integration of habits of coöperation among free men in work and play and battle, and was dimmed and extinguished when these habits were vacated by the impulsions of life for other channels.

To the Romans, unsuccessful in developing coöperative freedom on their own, what had been a life among the Greeks became a doctrine and a discipline, a sorrowful and artificial grafting of an alien ideal upon the native life, with the aliency ever apparent and vocal in conduct and in literature. For Hellenism was a decoration of the Roman way of life, not a part of its structure.

And so, it would seem, everywhere and always. Every unspent race or society is a dynamic character capable of a fullness and elaboration of life peculiar only to itself. Whatever discipline pertains to it is implicit in its process of fulfillment; whatever doctrine, in that fulfillment formulated as an ideal. Were only the world it lives in a place which was made for it, its progression from birth to culmination would be like the movement of a strain of music, continuous and complete. The world it lives in is, however, a place in which it merely happens, and whether this world's other denizens, also endowed with unique potencies pressing toward realization, favor or obstruct realization in their neighbors, is at no time law, is always accident and fortune. Accident and fortune are destiny, and if a hopeful observer of human life says, evil destiny, there is nothing in the variety and disorder of the species, the sporadic character of its freedom and achievements, the abundance of mutual repressions and thwartings, to say him nay.

Hence, when the liberties of men anywhere come to fruition in a good life, a culture of freedom and fellowship, this may become an ideal in those places where fruition has failed or is still on the way. There, men make of it a compensation in thought for the repressions and thwartings of their nature in fact. Its use is, to be an indicator of rebellion, pointing more truly that against which the spirit revolts than that toward which it turns. When such a revolt is successful and energies have truly broken free, they do not rest in compensatory ideals. The alien vision is absorbed by the freed society as food is absorbed by the body, and in a like manner transmuted. It becomes then flesh of the society's flesh, spirit of its spirit. That which it was a reaction against and a compensation for is forgotten. That toward which it turned becomes a program and an instrument in the winning of new life. Ideals cease to be compensatory and become expressive. Between them and the life which realizes them the aliency has disappeared. The two are now a continuous whole, potency and actuality foreshadowed and fulfilled, one in the other. The moment of this fulfillment, more or less complete, incarnates the genius of the age or race. When it passes, when it ceases to be a life and becomes a memory, it is enshrined in the schools as doctrine and discipline, compensatory once more, a spiritual cul-de-sac, an impasse of the mind, not only not humane, but anti-human.

So it has been with the Humanism of tradition which the schools proclaim and reverence. This, too, is a particular device, an instrument which modern Europe fashioned from antique materials to pattern for itself new life and more life and better life. Quite other is the underlying Humanism of history. That, from the Greeks to the Romantic lovers of Greek excellence, appears as the recurrent and cumulative endeavor by which outworn customs, doctrines, *mores,* taboos, prescriptions, standards, ideals, riding

mankind like an incubus, are thrown off and
abandoned, or subdued into agents and engines
of life once more, as, out of the Renaissance, religion was subdued and feudalism abandoned.
By force of this endeavor races and generations
of men grow, according to their kind, into the
freedom and fellowship appropriate to the diverse individualities that compose them, autonomous and coöperative at once, as Florence became during the Renaissance, and many a busy
city, south and north.   Freedom and fellowship
are the qualities in which this Humanism is best
manifest; it exists where they obtain.   It brings
forth out of itself the doctrine and discipline
proper to the race and generation it expresses,
and these are as new as the form of society is unprecedented.   They follow from the inwardness
of personality and institution that compose the
new society, and nothing else beside.   And where
any person or any community attempts to impose upon itself an alien law, from an alien time
or place, even the times and places of its own
lapsed story (as some Jews hope, in Palestine,
to reëstablish the ritual fullness of the Torah), it
meets the fate of the fabled frog that would be
an ox.

There are signs, in spite of horror, in spite of
the humiliations of the "price-system" and the
retrogression of war, that a fresh phase of this

perennial Humanism is beginning, the phase of
our industrial age. There are signs, faint signs
and perhaps transitory, yet it cannot be that they
are without ground in the dynamic units of our
machine culture, and that they will not grow
into the excellences of association in work and
play which those units portend. At the moment,
the signs are still too much in the form of disaffection and compensation. Consider the attitude of the Genro of Rebellious Youth. They
accept industry, but they repudiate the economic
Calvinism by which the beneficiaries of industry
rationalize the degradation of the time as the
permanent condition of progress. They denounce the apologetics which the academic clients
of the beneficiaries prepare as orthodox political
and social science. They deny the validity of this
soi-disant science and reject its discipline in field
and factory no less than in the colleges. Toward the counter-orthodoxy of socialism and its
derivatives they show more tolerance but equal
distaste. The things they happen to affirm—
e. g., European refinements of sensibility and
discipline—themselves are set in antithesis to the
things they reject. Everything turns upon the
industrial economy, its import and effects. Its
contagion has been transfused to all the reaches of
human life. The economic motive is used now
to explain all conduct; to light up the "new his-

tory" like a dark lantern; to supply the elemental presuppositions of the "new" sciences of man. And these, again, have been used mainly to justify or attack the domain of capitalistic industry in which they arose and grew. Literature and the fine arts, on the other hand, at least throughout the brief century of the growth of capitalistic industry into dominion and empire, have been reactions against and compensations for it, all the populous way from the Pre-Raphaelites to the Symbolists, from the Impressionists to the Futurists.

They continue so. Yet, as the 20th century gathers headway, the men of the industrial age begin to presage a reconciliation with their own handiwork. It is suggested in the very warfare of the classes, once so subterranean, with all law and all power on the side of the masters, all insecurity on the side of the men; now open, with the field fairer and the favor less, a code of right developing—as in the case of the garment industry in America—out of the dynamics of interest in the industry itself. It is suggested in the secure dignity and power of the great coöperative societies of Britain and Belgium, societies in which industry itself acts as the focus of freedom and fellowship. It is suggested, in spite of propaganda, in the turn the "social sciences" have taken away from apologetics and attacks to understanding. There is movement—as of a glacier in its slowness, a cloud in its vagueness, but movement—from partisanship to comprehension, from comprehension to mastery. Straker, the chauffeur in Shaw's *Man and Superman,* may be taken as a prophecy of one of the stations of this movement, whose terminal would be harmony between the new works and the ancient heart of man, and all whose steps are an endeavor to turn the uses of adversity toward the joy and tranquillity of the soul. Understanding is its prerequisite, a new Humanism its consummation.

III

The living pattern of this new Humanism, the Humanism of the industrial age, cannot yet be fully prefigured. Only some of its qualities can be signalized and the attitude toward man and the world in which its freedom and fellowship cohere. Could people but turn their sentiments more swiftly and knowingly from what industry defeats to what industry creates; could they, without distorting, accept its promptings toward associative forms and personal integrity; could they, in short, substitute intelligent self-direction for passional response, the humanization of industry would be more like a free adjustment and

a happy growth than a foolish struggle and a
deformed urge toward the boundless air and
the sun. But because our bodies change so
much more slowly than our minds, our ways of
thinking, our habits, our skills, survive the
objects of thought that called them forth and
fulfilled them, and when new objects come,
making for us a new mind, these old ways remain, irrelevant yet controlling. Against their
inertia and established rule, the new objects make
but slow headway, as inevitably they evoke new
skills, habits and ways of thought appropriate
to themselves. These latter appear sporadically
in the body-politic, divided in time and place,
unintegrated as yet into a single way of living
which is a culture and whose perfection is Humanism. It is these strange sporadic novelties
that can be observed and signalized, and from
which can be gathered some hint or prophecy of
the good to come. For it is a good that comes,
Rebellious Youth to the contrary notwithstanding. Whatever comes, that comes in self-
fulfillment, with its future a perfection and not
a distortion of its past, is a good. It has been
loyal to its own nature and actualized its inevitable ideal. Often it is accompanied by con-
tingencies and excrescences that make a braver
show and a greater noise, but they are irrelevant
or inimical—pure negations, as in times of read-

justment, like the times current, so many things
are. Meanwhile the good of things grows, and
all that promises it, whatever by just existing
prophesies it, makes light and leading. It is these
that must be discerned.

Fortunately, their gleam is not too beclouded.
The industrial economy which generates them
itself requires a favorable ground and environment, which it cannot have originated and without which it cannot continue. This ground and
environment is an inexorable presumption also
for the new Humanism itself. The usual name
for it is Science. As *milieu* and atmosphere of
the industrial community it is, however, something more subtle, more pervasive and altera-
tive than the interests and achievements of its
special disciplines in schools and factories. It is
a posture of the mind, a pattern of organic behavior, at once fluid and tensile, insinuating itself into all the enterprises of man, offsetting
earlier and deeper and more passionate attitudes
by the comminuted range and intimacy of its
penetrations, so that it dissolves the innermost
rigidities of every conception it touches, and
every faith. Originating in the Renaissance
flood of human energies as one of the innumerable manners of adventure whereof the Renaissance was so largely constituted, it survived as a
habit and skill of the mind and developed for

itself a technology of hypothesis, experiment, measurement and verification which has become a dominant institution of civilized society with constantly more adequate tools and constantly richer and more varied materials of operation. Its biologic mode is curiosity; its drive, whatever impulse sets it free to satisfy its own hungers. Thus, both war and peace have enlarged it and been tributary to it, for the scientist at work has had to be enfranchised from the very preoccupations that set him his problem that he might the more fully absorb himself in the matter of the problem alone. For this reason, the utilities of modern culture arise out of science and return into it; it is the place of coincidence of instruments and ends. And because Science is this, it dissolves also the perspectives of value which are the be-all and end-all of field and factory, church, legislature and school. What enters its domain enters a metaphysical democracy. All items of experience, regardless of their status in the other institutions of society, receive in that domain equal recognition of their integrity, equal regard.

And this holds true whether of the sciences of things or of the sciences of man. The psychologic disciplines also, as they pass from speculation to observation, from appreciation to measurement, from mythology to positive knowledge, diminish in favoritism and superstition and lay profane hands upon all the sacred cows of civilization, even patriotism and capital, even the proletarian and labor. Science thus, rather than death, is the great leveller, for it levels without destroying, it levels and liberates. Its revelations of fact dissolve and wash away the prerogatives of classes, the presumptions of special civilizations, all the false perspectives of the arts of man. Each man, any man, each society, any society, each episode of human experience, becomes a thing of inviolable integrity, a center of values, and a proper theme for the artist and philosopher.

Inevitably, in view of its structure and process, the machine of industry gives concentration and point to the temper of Science. The machine simultaneously divides and unites men, for it separates a single act of production into many mechanical steps, each step with a worker to mind it, and all the workers dependent on each other in the degree in which the labor of the single act of production is divided. So the machine makes directly for diversity and coöperation, which become humane as they become conscious and organic in the workers. So also, it invites equality, for in a process of production where every step is an ineluctable essential to the completion of the act, no claim can long be successfully maintained for the greater importance of any one step, as the slow but undeviating movement of trade-union practices from craft toward industrial organization attests. Indeed, the story of the workers' associations, the trade-unions and the coöperative societies, and of the theories and philosophies which envision them, is direct witness of the pressure toward diversity, equality and coöperation in the domain of the industrial machine. They are further favored by the contraction of distance through the facilitation of transport which the tremendously elaborated tools of our machine age have effected, to the point that London is nearer to Calcutta or New York to Pekin, than either was to Glasgow or Washington a century ago. And this in its turn has reënforced industry in directing masses of men from a sedentary to a mobile habit of life, so that hardly any men of an industrial society live where they were born or work at what they were trained for. The circle is complete, thus; a vicious circle as those who go its dreary round and those who resent the going see it. Let them, however, follow its true bent, and it may become the Platonic circle of perfection. Within it, peoples, cultures, races, religions, become swift neighbors. Strangers cease to be strange, aliens become familiar without ceasing to be different. The misunderstandings of aliency wear down. Contact generates tolerance.

Men learn to respect difference, to mitigate the instinctive demand for conformity. Peoples of diverse origin, habits and standards are more at home with one another. Industry and its derivatives have rendered them more interdependent and the world-wide integration of societies which it has effected, in the competition, it is true, for empire, nevertheless repudiates this competition and slowly compels the conduct of governments and ideals of peoples to congruity with the basic facts of industrial life.

Is it a too hopeful reading of these signs to say that industry tends of its own momentum to generate its proper *ethos,* that it moves, painfully, and with much labor, toward its own harmonious pattern of freedom and fellowship, its own Humanism?

If it be, what reading is to be given to the spirit of the new generation, the new temper of the arts?

Ah, this new generation! Its quality is more articulate in its women than its men; the mutation from past types is in them more radical, more stable. With the men the continuity is strained but not broken; their change was easier because their freedom had been greater. But, men and women, the new generation is here in mass, a theme for lamentation or gratulation in sermon and story, yet far from being quite

undisturbed in itself, and altogether disturbing
to even its wisest elders. Let us look at it for a
moment as a sensitive and photographic writer
sees it. I quote from Miss Edna Ferber's vivid
black and white study of three mid-continental
generations, *The Girls.*

"A slim, pliant, young thing this Charley, in
her straight dark blue frock. She was so mis-
leadingly pink and white and golden that you
neglected to notice the fine brow, the chin squar-
ish in spite of its soft curves, the rather deep-
set eyes. From her perch Charley's long brown-
silk legs swung. You saw that her stockings
were rolled neatly and expertly just below knees
as bare and hardy as a Highlander's. . . . A
young woman who belonged to the modern school
that despises sentiment and frowns upon weakly
emotional display; to whom rebellion is a normal
state; clear-eyed, remorseless, honest, fearless,
terrifying; the first woman since Eve to tell the
truth and face the consequences." The men are
not quite up to it, but not far behind. "Charley
commanded whole squads of devoted young men
in assorted sizes, positions and conditions.
Young men who liked country hikes, and way-
side lunches; young men who preferred to dance
at the Blackstone on Saturday afternoons;
young men who took Charley to the symphony
concerts; young men who read to her out of

books. . . . A lean-flanked, graceful crew they were, for the most part, with an almost feline co-ordination of muscle. When they shook hands with you their grip drove the rings into your fingers. They looked you in the eyes—and blushed a little. Their profiles would have put a movie star to shame. Their waists were slim as a girl's (tennis and baseball). They drove cars around Hyde Park corners with death-defying expertness. Nerveless; not talkative yet well up on the small talk of the younger set— labor, socialism, sex, baseball, Freud, psychiatry, dancing. . . ."

The point is there, in "the small talk of the younger set." There has been a stripping away of masks, stratagems, and evasions interposed between the young and the exigencies and routine of existence. There has been a concentration on the attainment of self-knowledge and self-mastery through the psychological disciplines; not constrained; spontaneous rather, and inevitable. Its spirit is a joyous realism. There are no illusions in it, except the illusions natural to youth. It aims at freedom but its foundations are such that when it turns from rebellion to creation the freedom it attains will rest secure on the recognition of the causal bases of life and will crave the courageous attempt to evaluate and master them.

Something of similar quality is apparent in the arts, particularly in poetry. Their themes are now drawn from any range and walk of life and any portion of the world. Their forms move outstandingly toward simplicity and flexibility. Their moods strive after sincerity and naturalism, but after a true naturalism, not the naturalism of Zola or the late Victorians. That was a metaphysics of matter applied to the portrayal of mankind. Its mood was despair and it celebrated the ugly as alone the good. It had no heart for joy and no eye for beauty. This is an experiential naturalism. It acquiesces in the living propulsions of its theme. It seeks to understand it by its history and setting and to give it ideal fulfillment by working out the perfections wherein a reaction to life becomes an achievement of art. Both joy and beauty enter into it. Its best exemplification that I know is Knut Hamsun's *Growth of the Soil.* But it is occasionally observable in the works of Robert Frost, of Carl Sandburg, of Vachel Lindsay, and many others, even Amy Lowell and James Cabell. It is adequate in the vertical architecture which strangers distinguish at once as the new characteristic expression of our industrial community and which does perhaps more completely than any other art bring to fruition the potencies of its material in the actualities of its form.

To this new naturalism, which may turn out
to be just the old classicism in an atmosphere
of science and democracy, the common and familiar and the rare and strange are on the same
level. It does not interpret, it envisages. The
metaphysical democracy of science directs its
imagination and guides its craftsmanship. Before its temper and spirit the ancestral quarrel of
romanticists and classicists, of ancients and moderns, is dispelled as vapor before sunlight. History and the future, the near and the far, the
passionate and the intellectual, the traditional
and the novel, the ephemeral and the lasting, the
hidden as well as the public, have equal holiday
in its court, but particularly the hitherto unregarded common things, the routine and grubby
detail of the daily life. Whatever has a ground
in existence is capable of a glow of beauty without illusion, which this new spirit in art promises
to elicit and set forth—even war, if Henri Bar-
busse's *Under Fire* has any import in this matter. You cannot anywhere touch the art of letters, which is the most representative of the arts
and most significant of the trend of the race,
without receiving from it a sure presentiment regarding the oneness of the mood and the diversity of the themes of the new age. . . .

So the perennial protean Humanism casts its

beams before, sends its forerunners, heralds and
trumpeters as once again its protean nature ad-
vances in new guise, with industry for body and
science for soul. It promises, when it comes, to
be much more socialized than the old Humanism,
its freedom and fellowship being spelled in terms
of the community in the individual, not the individual in the community. Of religion, in its traditional sense, it gives no indication; it would
seem to make no claims on life; rather it accepts
and enjoys. Its spirit, consequently, will be
catholic, tolerant, disillusioned and serene. It
will be what Buddhism would have been, had it
acquiesced in all desires and acknowledged the
existential parity of each with each, rather than
denied all. For civilized freedom is nearer to
Nature as self-acquiescence than as self-rejec-
tion. With self-acquiescence, the lines of the life
of civilization and the courses of Nature are
continuous, and wisdom, which is the art of living, becomes simply the coördination and ordering of impulsions with one another, and with the
conditions of their existence and satisfaction.
Such is the wisdom that the new Humanism
presages. It is a wisdom which seems like to
cherish neither regrets nor fears, whose hope will
arise out of knowledge, and faith out of understanding. It will be compact of the courage and
contentment of disillusion, of the love and the joy

of the beauty of common things. Largely and vaguely Walt Whitman had premonitions of such a wisdom; William James lived in its shadow. In the younger generation it is an occasional rare event, recurring slowly with less infrequency.

THE END

THE END